CAPABILITY BROWN

CAPABILITY BROWN

THE STORY OF A MASTER GARDENER

THOMAS HINDE

HUTCHINSON

LONDON MELBOURNE AUCKLAND JOHANNESBURG

Author's Note

It is impossible to imagine a biographer of Capability Brown who would not be indebted to Dorothy Stroud. Her pioneer work on Brown mapped the field and no one is ever likely to redraw its broad outline. True, I have found new evidence, and sometimes come to different conclusions, but my aim was never to write a new version of her comprehensive book. Instead, by concentrating on a selection of Brown's numerous works, and by giving some attention to his employers as well as to their properties, I have tried to create a fuller idea of his problems and how he dealt with them, and as a result bring him more to life as a person. In parallel with this I have hoped to bring to life the society which formed the man, and to whose artistic impulses he in turn gave shape.

Text © Thomas Hinde 1986
Photographs by Timothy Beddow (as specified on page 220)
Illustrations by Emma Tovey

First published in Great Britain in 1986 by Century Hutchinson Ltd,
Brookmount House, 62-65 Chandos Place, Covent Garden, London WC2N 4NW

Century Hutchinson Publishing Group (Australia) Pty Ltd
16-22 Church Street, Hawthorn, Melbourne, Victoria 3122

Century Hutchinson (NZ) Ltd
32-34 View Road, PO Box 40-086, Glenfield, Auckland 10

Century Hutchinson Group (SA) Pty Ltd
PO Box 337, Bergvlei 2012, South Africa

Designed and produced by Robert Ditchfield Ltd
Typeset by Oxford Computer Typesetting
Printed and bound in Hong Kong by Mandarin Offset Ltd

ISBN 0 09 163740 6

Contents

1. Lancelot 'Capability' Brown by Nathaniel Dance, *c.* 1768

Introduction

LANCELOT 'CAPABILITY' BROWN's work was the triumphant climax of a revolution which transformed the art of gardening in the eighteenth century and gave the world the term *le jardin anglais*.

Almost a hundred years before Brown was born, the first stirrings of this revolution can be found in Francis Bacon's essay on gardening (1625) in which he asked for wild places in a garden; but during the rest of the century gardens became increasingly formal. English gardeners copied French, in particular André le Nôtre, creator of Versailles, and exiled Royalists who returned to England after the restoration of 1660 were keen to imitate him.

The engravings of Kip and Knyff give the best impression of the result. They show great house after great house surrounded by canals, fountains, topiary, avenues of clipped trees and extensive beds of flowers, shrubs, and gravels. In 1688, when William III became king, some gardens were modified to imitate those of the Netherlands (more complex topiary, lead statues, trees in tubs, box hedges and flowering bulbs), but the general effect remained rigidly formal. In these years it seemed that the art of gardening had reached an ultimate and definable perfection.

But from the early 1700s poets and critics like Alexander Pope and Joseph Addison began to deplore both the formality and the uniformity of such gardens. A garden, they argued, should not be imposed indiscriminately on a piece of land but should consult the genius of the place. 1719 is often said to mark the first translation of such theories into practice because this was the year in which the young painter and future landscape designer, William Kent, returned from Italy to England with his patron, Lord Burlington. If the period of change which followed is divided into two, the next thirty years were Kent's, and the succeeding thirty Brown's.

Kent did what the new taste in gardening demanded, what his experiences of Italy and of paintings of the Italian landscape suggested, and what technical developments like the ha-ha allowed. Modern taste demanded the abolition of formal beds, clipped avenues and 'foolish waterworks'; Italy and its painters suggested garden temples, monuments and ruins; the ha-ha allowed the irregularities of nature into the garden and improvements into the surrounding park. Stowe in Buckinghamshire is the most famous of the gardens to which Kent applied his designs. And the story of Brown's work begins precisely where Kent's ends: in this magnificent, ornament-littered garden, to which Kent contributed so much and where Brown became head gardener.

The landscapes Brown designed were costly. Unless his clients had been enormously rich his plans could never have been carried out. Since national peace and prosperity often go together, it is easy to forget that the years of Brown's working life were far from peaceful. In 1745 while he was at Stowe an invading Scottish army almost threw the Hanoverians off the throne. For twenty-five out of the forty-four years between his arrival in the south and his death, England was at war either with continental enemies or with her American colonies. The remarkable thing is how little these wars and the turbulent political events which accompanied them affected Brown's professional life. In office or out, come peace or war, the great landowners of England wanted and were able to afford the sort of grandiose parks which Brown made for them.

This is not to say that Brown's work was uninfluenced by the politics of his time. The opposite is true. Certainly he had many Tory clients, but those who gave him strongest support were the Whig 'patriots'. To them his style of gardening was important, first because it was native-born and owed nothing to foreign example, but more importantly because it symbolized the new freedom in which they believed. The restraints and rigidities of continental practice were banished, and in their place Brown provided sweeping landscapes of trees, lakes and lawns where the noblemen of England could drive, ride and breathe the free English air. As a result, our ideas of what should constitute a great garden have never again been the same.

2. Audley End, Essex.

1. Northumberland

TWO HUNDRED AND SEVENTY years ago, in the Northumberland hamlet of Kirkharle, a boy to be called Lancelot Brown was born, fifth child of six in his family. Kirkharle lies in the valley of the Wansbeck. It is remote enough today, echoing to the bleating of sheep on the nearby moors. In the early eighteenth century it would have been more so.

The hamlet consisted of a cluster of small stone houses set on low ground close to one branch of a tributary of the Wansbeck known as the Kirkharle Burn. Nearby stood Kirkharle Tower, home of Sir William Loraine, owner of the village and surrounding lands. During Brown's lifetime the village was moved to a more fitting distance, half a mile to the south-west. But its communal field, with the characteristic ridges and furrows of mediaeval strip farming can still be seen near the earlier site. Its church, St Wilfrid's, also survives, though today its services are monthly and its graveyard a sheep pen. It stands on higher ground to the north. Since 1983 a plaque on the wall of the nave has commemorated the baptism here of Lancelote Browne (as the parish register has it) on 16 August 1716.[1] This was the child who, during the next sixty-seven years, was not only to transform the grounds of the great houses of almost two hundred of the country's leading families, but to establish in the process a style of landscaping which permanently changed our ideas about the delights of nature.

Of Brown's father and mother almost nothing is known. (It is not even certain whether or not they normally spelt Brown with an 'e'. In later life Lancelot didn't, though his clients occasionally did.) According to the Revd John Hodgson, who published his history of Northumberland some hundred years later, the family were of yeoman stock, and came from Ravenscleugh in nearby Redesdale.[2] But Lancelot's branch had lived at Kirkharle for some time. A Dorothy Browne and a Lancelot Browne, probably young Lancelot's grandparents, died there in 1699 and 1700 respectively. And the births of Lancelot's brothers and sisters are duly recorded in succession. First, two sisters were born in 1704 and 1706, then two brothers, John and George, who were baptized in 1708 and 1713. Then came Lancelot, baptized in 1716, and finally in 1719 another sister.[3]

But already there are mysteries. There is no mention of the marriage of Lance-lot's father William to his mother; and nowhere in any of these entries in the parish register is Lancelot's mother's Christian name given.

It is also somewhat surprising that a boy of his social class should have stayed at school, as he did, until he was sixteen. He would have gone first to the village school, but of that there is no record. Presently he transferred to the school at Cambo, two miles away.[4] To this he must have walked daily, not by today's road, but by a path which forded the Wansbeck then passed to the west of Wallington Hall, the great house of Sir Walter Calverley Blackett (with whom he was involved many years later). At Cambo his school can hardly have been inspiring. The small compact stone village was only a little larger than Kirkharle, and the local parson was probably the teacher.

Almost everything else that is known about the first twenty-three years of Lancelot Brown's life is connected with Kirkharle Tower, and with its owners, Sir William and Lady Loraine. As soon as Brown left school they engaged him to work for them in their vegetable garden. It was certainly Brown's job with the Loraines that first gave him a serious interest in gardening. But his early position there, in the vegetable garden, has suggested to many that his career is a classic poor-boy-makes-good story, and writers have connected him with vegetable gardening long after he had anything to do with it. The mistake is ironic, because of all the great gardeners, Brown was the least a plantsman. Trees and shrubs he valued and he was probably knowledgeable about them, but there is so little evidence that he was interested in flowers, let alone vegetables, that the opposite can be presumed. There could even be a connection between his first job and the way, in landscape after landscape, he moved the vegetable garden away from the house to some remote and inconvenient corner of the grounds.

At this time Sir William Loraine was making improvements to Kirkharle on a large scale. He had inherited the estate in 1718 at the age of sixty, and during the next twenty-five years he rebuilt various derelict parts of St Wilfrid's church, giving the 'quire' a stone floor instead of an earthen one, and 'built a new mansion-house (of his own plan and contrivance) with all the offices, out-houses, gardens, fountains, fish-ponds etc. (the first regular ones ever made in that county) belonging to them.' According to the same contemporary account he was 'compe-tent in judgement of architecture and physick, exemplary in planting and inclo-sure; having from the year 1694 to 1738 inclusive, planted of forest-trees twenty-four thousand, and of quick-sets above four hundred and eighty-eight thousand, and being skilful in the fruit gardens, planted of fruit-trees five hundred and eighty.'[5]

Brown's later career has always made it tempting to suggest that he was involved in much of this work, and there is evidence, again from Hodgson, that he could have been. Before he left the north he was borrowed by Mr Shafto of Benwell, on the outskirts of Newcastle.[6] Loraine would hardly have lent Shafto a vegetable-garden boy. This loan of Brown to another garden owner is more

3. Kirkharle Hall, from Sir Lambton Loraine, Bt, *Pedigree and Memoirs of the Family of Loraine of Kirkharle* (1902).

probably an early parallel to the loaning of Brown by Cobham of Stowe, his most important early employer in the south, to various friends to help them improve their estates.

Finally, in 1739 Brown left Northumberland, probably with an introduction to Lady Loraine's family in Buckinghamshire, which in due course secured him work down there. Such has been the generally accepted story of the rise of a poor village boy towards success. His genius, it seems, came from nowhere.

But there is evidence that the Brown family's connection with the Loraines was, at the very least, much closer. Four years after Lancelot left for the south, on 23 April 1743, his older brother, John, married Jane Loraine, Sir William's youngest daughter. Jane was forty, perhaps a good enough reason for the Loraine family to accept John Brown as a son-in-law. Sir Lambton Loraine, who published a family history in 1902, speculates that 'This apparently strange marriage... seems to have had some sanction in the great brilliancy of the gardener's career.'[7] But by 1743 Brown's career had hardly yet the sort of brilliance which would have much influenced them.

Lambton Loraine adds that John Brown subsequently became the Loraine's steward. He does not, however, comment on the fact that one Jn° Brown was a witness to Sir William Loraine's will in 1734, to a codicil to a lost will in 1739 and to a memorandum to the codicil in 1740.[8] If this John was Lancelot's brother — there are not likely to have been two John Browns at Kirkharle in the 1730s — he was by this time closely connected with the Loraine household, if not already the steward. He could have been working at the hall in 1732 when the Loraines first employed his young brother, Lancelot, in their garden.

There is a more interesting possible explanation of young Lancelot's early rise in his profession. According to local tradition, his mother worked as a servant at the hall and Lancelot was Sir William Loraine's illegitimate son. This story was passed to the Revd J.K. Young by his predecessor, Canon A.H. Walker, vicar of Kirkharle from 1960 to 1979, and can be traced no further back.[9] But if it is correct, many surprising things seem less so. Most obviously, if Brown was Sir William's natural son, it is no longer odd that a Northumberland village family should suddenly produce a boy of genius. Nor, since Sir William had a particular interest in, and talent for, gardening and architecture, that Brown should also have had these talents and interests. Nor, if Loraine was taking a special interest in the boy, that he should have kept him at school till he was sixteen, then employed him, quickly promoted him and finally when he had taught him his trade, have sent him south with a letter of introduction to relatives there.

Apart from local tradition and circumstantial evidence of this sort, the theory could be best supported by comparing portraits of Brown with those of the Loraines who would then be his father (Sir William), his half brother (Sir Charles), and his four other half brothers, and seeing a resemblance. Unfortunately no such portraits have yet been found, and it must be admitted that those of later Loraines show no particular likeness.

A separate tradition has long held that Brown's departure in 1739 was not the end of his professional connection with Kirkharle, but that he returned in the 1760s or 1770s to work for another Sir William, grandson of the first. It was then, according to Hodgson, that 'the magic hand of Brown contrived to throw the sweetest charms into the fields of the place of his nativity, and to convert the landscape around the mansion of their lord into a "woody theatre of stateliest view"'.[10]

Recently an important new piece of evidence has been discovered which has generally been taken to confirm that Brown did indeed return to work again for the Loraines.[11] A few years ago John Anderson, whose family bought Kirkharle from the Loraines in 1832, found among his grandfather's papers a plan for improving Kirkharle.[12] Though this is unsigned, its style proves it to be almost certainly Brown's. It shows the Kirkharle Burn dammed and expanded into a sinuous lake, a peripheral belt of trees enclosing a park set with typical Brown-like clumps, and a characteristic double drive circling towards the hall rather than approaching it directly.

This so-called plan of the 1760s or 1770s may have a far greater significance than

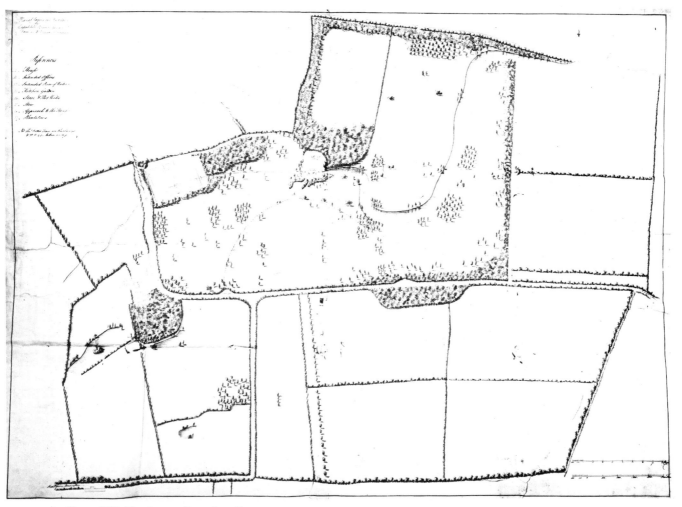

4. Plan of Kirkharle, attributed to Brown.

has formerly been supposed, for it could have been drawn as early as the 1730s, before Brown ever left Northumberland.

The dating of the new Brown plan depends on deciding whether it shows the old tower at Kirkharle or the new hall, and on dating the replacing of the one by the other. The present Kirkharle Farm is a surviving part of the new hall — a nineteenth century painting reproduced by Sir Lambton Loraine (see page 11) leaves no doubt that this is so. But a study of the landscape and a careful comparison of the position of this farm/hall with the position of the building Brown shows, suggest that Brown's lies slightly to the west. Moreover, the shape and size of Brown's building — two modest semi-detached squares — suggest not a gentleman's new mansion house but a defensive peel-tower of the sort common in these parts.

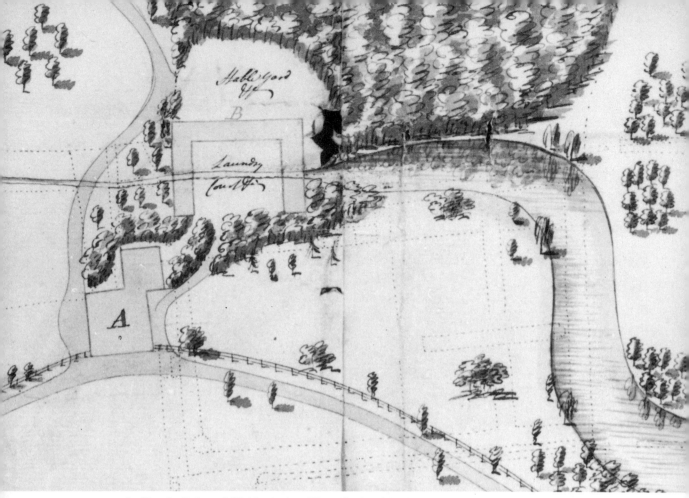

5. Detail of plan of Kirkharle (see Plate 4), showing the house (probably the old Kirkharle Tower which was demolished) and offices (probably those which survive the farm buildings).

So when was this tower replaced? Both Sir Williams built extensively. About the second, who inherited Kirkharle in 1755 at the age of five or six, Hodgson writes that he 'new roofed the body of the house, added two wings, and a suite of offices behind, and removed the fountains and gardens of his grandfather, but preserved the tall forest trees which shelter and diversify the adjoining ground, and drained the flat land on the north side of the house, the situation of which is low and shaded by a hill to the south'.[13]

Hodgson was not always accurate, but here he is describing a part of the country he knew well. He was for many years vicar of Kirkwhelpington, then of Hartburn which both lie close to Kirkharle.[14] It was clearly his opinion that the second Sir William repaired and extended Kirkharle, but not that he built an entirely new hall.

John Wallis, another Northumberland clergyman, confirms this. He visited Kirkharle around 1768 and wrote of the second Sir William: 'His seat is in a low situation; rebuilt by his grandfather, Sir William'.[15] And the account quoted above of the first Sir William's building and gardening at Kirkharle, which was printed during his lifetime in 1740, specifically says that it was he who built a new mansion-house.

The evidence therefore strongly suggests that Brown's plan shows the old tower, and that it was the first Sir William who replaced this with the new hall, moving it slightly to the east. And he apparently did so before 1740. It is difficult to avoid the deduction that Brown's plan was therefore drawn in the 1730s, and that it represents a proposal made when the first Sir William was still intending to preserve the old tower. Could it perhaps have been an exercise in landscaping which he set his young protégé? If so, the first Sir William Loraine was a far more important influence on Brown than has previously been realized.

6. St Wilfrid's Church, Kirkharle, where Brown was baptized on 16 August 1716.

7. Lord Cobham of Stowe, after J.B. van Loo.

2. Stowe

 BROWN ALMOST CERTAINLY arrived in the south of England with an introduction to one of Lady (Anne) Loraine's relations. She had been born Anne Smith and members of her family still lived in Buckinghamshire, close enough to the places where Brown soon found work to make this connection highly likely. The Smiths who most probably helped Brown were Anne's brother, Richard of Enderby, or her (probable) nephew, Richard of Padbury. The son of the former eventually left his land to the grandson of Sir William Loraine, Brown's earliest employer, proving that these Smiths remained closely connected with their Northumberland relatives.[1]

Precisely which of them helped Brown to find a job is not known. Nor is it entirely certain what this first job was. It was once believed to have been at Wotton, seat of Sir Richard Grenville. There were circumstantial reasons for thinking so. Richard Grenville was the nephew of Lord Cobham of Stowe, the great garden to which Brown moved two years later. A job with Grenville could naturally have led to a job with Cobham and Brown did indeed later work at Wotton.

But the best account of Brown's early years in the south implies that he was first employed by Sir Charles Browne (no relation) at Kiddington, an Oxfordshire house lying four and a half miles north-west of Woodstock. This version of events was described as the most probable as early as 1827 by Hodgson in his history of Northumberland,[2] where he correctly credits it to John Penn's book, *An Historical and Descriptive Account of Stoke Park*.[3]

John Penn lived at Stoke House, which was in the same county as Stowe, and had close connections with it. Here Lady Cobham retired from Stowe when her husband died in 1749. And Penn sent a copy of his book to the Honourable Thomas Grenville of Wotton (now the British Library's copy). It is most unlikely that he would have incorrectly deprived Wotton of the credit for first employing Brown in the south.

When Penn reaches the point at which Brown prepared a plan for Stoke (as he did in 1750), he inserts a brief biography: 'Brown was born... at a house, now no longer in existence, of the old village of Kirkharle parish... it has been said that the first piece of water he formed, was at Lady Mostyn's in Oxfordshire'.[4] This Lady Mostyn was Sir Charles Browne's grand-daughter, Barbara, who had married Sir Edward Mostyn and inherited Kiddington.

There are other reasons for believing Penn. Kiddington still looks like a Brown garden. Grassy slopes fall below the house to the south and west, where the little river Glyme has been dammed and turned into a modest lake. More grassy slopes rise fairly steeply on the further side where there are new clumps of trees as well as the stumps of much older ones. True, the valley's shape made the river easy to dam, and its slopes invited lawns and trees, but that is all the more reason for thinking that Brown may have seized the opportunity to make a garden which (apart from an encircling belt of trees) has most of the features of his numerous later ones.

John Penn next explains how Brown moved to Stowe:

It was, however, in consequence of an enquiry made near this time by Lord Cobham, from a nurseryman, whether he knew of anyone who could continue with him at Stowe, able to converse instructively on his favourite pursuit, but free from the vanity and conceit which had made his former assistants disinclined to alterations upon which he had determined, that Brown, already a landscape gardener, became an inmate of that princely mansion.[5]

8. Kiddington, Oxfordshire.

It would follow that the suggestion that Brown was first in charge of the vegetable gardens at Stowe, repeated if not originated by Horace Walpole,[6] is a highly improbable one. Cobham would hardly have put someone who was 'already a landscape gardener' into this position.

The period when Cobham would have been looking for a gardener 'to continue with him at Stowe', who could discuss his favourite subject with him, was February 1741, when William Love, the gardener who had been at Stowe since 1725, was leaving. The Stowe accounts show that Love was still there in this month, but from the second week of March 1741 the regular gardening bills were submitted to the Stowe steward by Brown. The first bundle is endorsed, 'The New Gardener's Bills', further evidence that Brown had just arrived. From this time onwards Brown was paid £25 a year, plus £9 boarding wages, exactly what Love had been paid. Like Love, he had thirty-five to forty gardeners under him.[7]

Lord Cobham, the great landowner who now became Brown's employer, was a sixty-five-year-old general, who had spent a good part of his early life campaigning abroad. Born Richard Temple, he had been made colonel of a new regiment of foot by William III, and fought for many years under Marlborough in the Netherlands and France. In 1708 he so distinguished himself at the siege of Lille that he was allowed to carry home personally the news of the city's surrender. His greatest success came eleven years later when he commanded the seaborne expedition sent to attack the north-west Spanish port of Corunna. Finding this too strongly defended he sailed on south and captured Vigo instead.

But Cobham's military career had been interrupted twice by his second interest: politics. As a Whig he had so fallen out of favour by 1713 that he was deprived of the command of his regiment. When George I came to the throne next year and the Whigs returned to power, he was made in turn a baron, a privy councillor, then a viscount.

He remained in favour till 1733 when his principles brought him into conflict with Walpole, the Prime Minister. He objected to Walpole's notorious excise bill, as well as to the protection Walpole was giving to the directors of the disastrous South Sea Company. Walpole caused a sensation by having Cobham dismissed again from his regiment. Such a thing had never been done to such an 'old and tried soldier'.[8] In reaction Cobham and other Whigs formed a faction known as the 'Patriots', which was presently joined by William Pitt, once a cornet in Cobham's regiment and soon to marry his niece.

In 1742 Cobham was promoted to Field Marshal, but the next year he finally resigned his commission because he objected to the use of British troops in support of Hanoverian interests in Europe.

For many years Cobham's military and political activities prevented him from indulging his third great interest: landscape gardening. Though he inherited the family estates in 1697 it was not till about 1713 that he began to garden actively at Stowe. Two years later, when he married Anne Halsey, the only daughter of a rich London brewer, he was able to garden more ambitiously, and even more so after

1719 when he received his share of the booty from the capture of Vigo. That winter, wagons from Stowe spent three days at Southampton collecting the loot.[9]

From then until the time of Brown's arrival, Cobham's gardens at Stowe were at the forefront of fashionable gardening. He employed in succession Charles Bridgeman and William Kent, the country's two leading gardeners. Bridgeman's great introduction at Stowe was the ha-ha. About the ha-ha's importance in general, Horace Walpole wrote:

> The capital stroke, the leading step to all that followed, was... the destruction of walls for boundaries, and the invention of fosses... No sooner was this simple enchantment made, than levelling, mowing, and rolling followed. The contiguous ground of the park without the sunk fence, was to be harmonized with the lawns within; and the garden in its turn was to be set free from its prim regularity, that it might assort with the wilder country without...[10]

Around 1720 ha-has were built in some half-a-dozen English gardens. George Clarke, Stowe's historian, claims that its own example could well have been the first. Not only were they often called fosses, but they were constructed much like military fosses, something which Cobham would have known about.[11] Inside the ha-ha, however, Bridgeman retained much of the geometric formality of a seventeenth-century garden. It was his successor at Stowe, William Kent, who deformalized the garden itself, making its many features irregular and natural.

The ideas which lay behind these changes are less easy to simplify. Today we judge a garden almost entirely by its 'look' — or very occasionally by its smell. In one sense Kent designed gardens to be judged in exactly the same way. He was a painter as well as a garden designer. He required his head gardeners to work 'without level or line' from pictures of the result he was aiming for.[12] And he was influenced by writers who believed that gardens should be pictures. Pope, one of the most important, wrote that 'all gardening is landscape painting'.

But the paintings which inspired Kent, and which he hoped his mature gardens would in real life grow to resemble, were not pure landscapes. They were those of the painters Poussin and Claude, in which the Italian landscape is decorated with classical ruins. Kent himself spent six years in Italy with his patron, Lord Burlington. In admiring the work of these painters, Kent was conforming to the general view of the time that, as Jonathan Richardson wrote in 1725, 'a history is preferable to a landscape, seascape, animals, fruit, flowers, or any other still-life, pieces of drollery, etc.'.[13]

'The reason is,' Richardson continued, 'the latter kinds may please... but they cannot improve the mind, they excite no noble sentiments.' The creation of garden features which improved the mind or excited noble sentiments was Kent's second aim, and it was by their success in doing this that they were judged.

A book of 1748 entitled *A Dialogue upon the Gardens of the Right Honourable the Lord Viscount Cobham at Stowe in Buckinghamshire* contains many examples of such judgements. In front of the Temple of British Worthies the guide says, 'Does not your

9. *A View from Capt. Grenville's Monument to the Grecian Temple* at Stowe, Buckinghamshire.

pulse beat high, while you thus stand before such an awful assembly? Is not your breast warmed by a variety of grand ideas, which this sight must give birth to?'.[14]

Addison's description of his 'Vision' in *The Tatler* of January 1710 may well have been the first inspiration for such garden features. He tells (somewhat immodestly) how he moved with a host of persons 'whose thoughts were bent upon doing eminent services to mankind, or promoting the good of their country', up a wooded valley lined with 'statues of lawyers, heroes, statesmen, philosophers and poets' towards a Temple of Virtue. Beyond this lay a Temple of Honour where a figure above the high altar was the Emblem of Eternity. Nearby was a Temple of Vanity where 'the stones were laid together without mortar... filled with hypocrites, pedants, free-thinkers, and prating politicians'.[15]

As Clarke has pointed out, the Elysian Fields at Stowe have all the main features of Addison's vision: 'A straight path (the Great Cross Lime Walk) is terminated by a Temple of Virtue (Ancient Virtue), beyond which lies a Temple of Honour (The British Worthies); nearby is a ruinous Temple of Vanity (Modern Virtue)'.[16]

Some of the garden buildings in what can loosely be called a Kent garden were meant to provoke other moods. Grottoes were to cause melancholy, ruins to cause nostalgia, and quaint cottages to surprise. All were scattered about the garden, forming no grand whole but to be discovered and create their particular effects individually. The garden, often called a pleasure garden, was where the owner or his friends would go for these experiences, a place quite apart from, often invisible from, the house. Stourhead in Wiltshire, made by its owner, the banker Henry Hoare, is the perfect example on a grand scale of a garden of this sort.

On the whole at Stowe, Kent worked for an employer who wanted his garden to evoke noble sentiments. And he wanted these to be of a particular kind. Just as Cobham's politics had influenced his military career, so they influenced his garden. To give just a few examples, his British Worthies — Drake, Raleigh, King Alfred, the Black Prince and others — represented, if some of them in more subtle ways, hostility to Walpole and support for the patriotic policies in which Cobham believed. The Temple of Modern Virtue, on the other hand, 'those poor shattered remains of what has never been very beautiful',[17] was 'designed to let us see the ruinous state of Modern Virtue', and included a headless statue of Cobham's chief political enemy, Walpole.[18] In the Temple of Friendship Cobham himself appeared together with William Pitt and other political allies.

Even the Gothic Temple, Clarke argues, had political significance. In the eighteenth century the word Gothic did not simply describe an architectural style, but was commonly used in the phrase 'our old Gothick constitution', considered to have been brought to us by invading Anglo-Saxon tribes who were loosely called Goths. It therefore 'came to imply all the moral and cultural values summed up in the term "Enlightenment".' These were what Cobham and his friends stood for, and the temple was dedicated 'To the Liberty of our Ancestors'.[19]

It was in a garden committed to such ideas that Brown worked for the next eight and a half years — until Cobham's death in September 1749. Kent may well have been absent most of the time — there is no firm evidence that he ever visited Stowe in the 1740s. Certainly Gibbs, the architect of the Gothic Temple, returned to design some of the garden temples and monuments which Brown built. But it was a Kent style garden that Brown was producing, because this was what Cobham wanted.

Thomas Whately's concluding verdict on Stowe gives a vivid picture of what the garden eventually became. It could hardly suggest a more emphatic contrast with the sort of landscapes which Brown was later to design:

> The multiplicity of the [buildings] has indeed been often urged as an objection to Stowe; and certainly when all are seen by a stranger in two or three hours, twenty or thirty capital structures, mixed with others of inferior note, do seem too many… if they are considered separately, at different times, and at leisure, it may be difficult to determine which to take away; yet still it must be acknowledged that their frequency destroys all ideas of silence and retirement.[20]

Apart from the restrictions which working in such a strong environment must have placed on Brown as a landscape gardener, a strange succession of accidents encouraged him to develop at Stowe in quite different directions. These accidents may well have made his later successes possible. They began almost at once.

The Stowe steward to whom he at first submitted his garden accounts was

William Roberts. But within six months Roberts was dead and gone. His death is described in a letter from a neighbour, Ralph Verney, of December 1741. Roberts, who was 'reputed an Atheist and a great favourite of Lord C.', had hanged himself soon after the assizes. He had apparently been so upset when Mr D. (presumably the assize judge) convicted a deer stealer that he had treated Mr D. 'not so civilly as he should', and when Cobham reprimanded him this 'vex'd him so much he made away with himself'.[21]

Roberts was replaced by Thomas Potts, but within a few months Leonard Lloyd, a Buckingham attorney who had the responsibility for providing cash for Stowe on Cobham's behalf, began to discover irregularities, and Potts finally disappeared in October 1742, together with a large sum of money. He is last heard of in an advertisement in *The Northampton Mercury*, offering ten guineas for information about 'where the said Potts may be found, so that he may be apprehended'.[22]

Lloyd now became steward at Stowe, but since he lived near the church in Buckingham, and no doubt because over the previous eighteen months Brown had proved reliable, Brown took on responsibilities far wider than those of a normal head gardener. He became in effect clerk of the works, and began to submit not merely gardening bills, but bills for all other work which was going on at Stowe. These included payments to carpenters, carters, sawyers, plasterers and masons, who at this time were busy with eight different projects. He was responsible for accounts for stone which was arriving from three quarries. Not surprisingly, by April 1747 he was no longer being referred to as the Gardener, but as Mr Brown.

10. Stowe: the view to the Corinthian Arch (designed by Thomas Pitt in 1765).

Nor would it be surprising if this was when the capable Mr Brown got his nickname.[23] Certainly he later used the word in the much-reported way, to suggest the 'capability' or potential of his clients' grounds, but it would be quite in character that he first started to use it to enjoy the joke of its double meaning.

It was logical that Brown's responsibility for building as well as gardening at Stowe should lead him to take a professional interest in architecture. He began to copy out from *The Builder's Dictionary or Gentleman's and Architect's Companion* his own glossary of architectural terms. Fifteen pages in his handwriting survive.[24] It was an exercise which demonstrated his ambition.

From a theoretical interest in architecture, Brown moved to taking a practical part. A note attached to a garden account of 1747 says that 'The plan of the Long Room' will be sent by the next post. 'I should have sent it this post but could not get it finished.'[25]

Meanwhile in the gardens he had been spending around £800 a year, not only building temples and monuments, but transforming Bridgeman's great parterre to the south of the house into a lawn and also thinning Bridgeman's woodlands. It was probably from these woodlands, now twenty years old, and also from formal avenues, that trees were taken for other parts of the gardens.

All gardeners who work with trees must accept the fact that their gardens will not become mature for many years, but not all have been resigned to this disadvantage, and various of them, the diarist John Evelyn included, had already devised methods of moving large trees. But they had been laborious and expensive, and when Brown was working at Stowe there had been no advance in the technique for about seventy years. Then with typical straightforwardness he invented a greatly improved tree-moving machine. It is easy to imagine him, faced with the convention of the day that large trees must be moved upright, making the original but at the same time obvious suggestion that they should be laid flat. He devised a machine which did just this. Henry Steuart described it in his *Planter's Guide*, first published in 1827.[26]

It consisted of a strong pole of considerable length, with two high wheels, and acting on an iron axle, which was placed at right angles to it. At the extremity of the pole there was a smaller wheel, that turned on a pivot, and was used for trees of more than ordinary magnitude... A strong cross-bow was bolted on the axle, with a space in the middle gradually hollowed out for receiving the stem of the tree... According to Brown's method, the top was pretty severely lopped or lightened, and sometimes quite pollarded. The roots were next cut round to the depth of the fibres, and only two or three feet out from the body, and the machine was brought up upon its wheels as close as possible to the tree. The pole was set upright, and applied to the stem, to which it was then lashed in the firmest manner. By a rope fixed at the top of the pole, it was, last of all, forcibly drawn down by several men's strength; and thus the stem and the pole of the machine, forming a lever of great power, forced or tore up the roots from their under-bed, with as many fibres adhering to them as escaped laceration.

11. The tree-moving machine from Sir Henry Steuart's *The Planter's Guide*, 1827.

This 'was no very gentle treatment of the roots', but Brown's 'genius was of that aspiring and ardent sort which fitted him rather for bold designs than minute detail and patient investigation' and he never studied trees carefully or, by implication, troubled to refine his somewhat crude method. Its great advantage was that it was quick and cheap. It did away with the crane and pulleys of earlier methods, as well as with the elaborate cutting of the outer roots a year or more in advance. As a result Brown could afford to move many more trees. Even if these were not enough for 'the execution of great outlines of wood', they were effective for the foreground and middle distance of the landscape.

As Steuart got his information from two of Brown's assistants, one of whom, James Robertson, 'was sent down to Scotland' about 1750, it seems certain that Brown invented his machine at Stowe. It remained an important tool of his trade for the next forty years. To garden historians it is equally important since it changes our picture of Brown landscapes in their early years. They would not have been planted entirely with saplings, but set about with transplants of between 15 and 36 feet. These were roughly the limits of those Steuart himself moved with a similar machine.

By the autumn of 1746 Brown had proved himself an efficient and trustworthy administrator, capable of carrying out all manner of building and gardening projects. He can be pictured at this time spending his days like any other administrator, in an office, at work on figures and calculations, plans and the logistics of carrying them out. Daily, perhaps more often, he would walk or ride about the

Stowe gardens checking the work of its teams of builders and gardeners.

The major works themselves would have looked more like battle-fields than garden features, particularly as they were usually undertaken in winter, when villagers were not needed in the fields and could be employed for 8d a day instead of 10d. This was also the season when the Cobhams were absent. They wintered in Hanover Square, only coming to Stowe from May to October. Then, in summer, Brown would accompany them about the grounds, explaining what had been done, listening to them plan new features. In summer Brown would have also had the duty of showing visitors round, thus making the aristocratic contacts which were to prove so useful to him. Then, as always, he must have impressed them with his competence, and pleased them with his properly deferential manner. Above all they found him likable.

But until now he had been given little opportunity at Stowe to develop the style of landscaping for which he became famous. In the autumn of 1746, however, Cobham began to create, in the north-east corner of the gardens, his last great garden feature, the Grecian Valley. In Christopher Hussey's opinion, the Grecian Valley is 'an important scene in the history of landscape architecture: the actual point of junction between Kent's and Brown's styles'.[27]

Hussey implies that for the first time Brown at least helped to design as well as to execute one of Stowe's major features. Certainly it was late for Kent to have designed it. He died in 1748 and is well known to have disliked travel even when younger. And certainly about the Grecian Valley there is the first piece of firm evidence that Brown was concerning himself with landscape design. It comes in a letter he wrote to Cobham, found folded in the gardening accounts of 24 February 1746. Brown writes:

> As to finishing the head of the oval I had never formed any other idea on it than what your Lordship gave me which was to forme the laurell plantation with a sweep under it and concave to the oval that the slope of the head your Lordship thought might some time or other have statues put on it, but gave me no absolute orders to finish it and indeed I think it would be better not finished this season I thinking that a summer's talk and tryels about it may make it a very fine thing.[28]

This letter is of the greatest interest because, as well as suggesting the part Brown played in designing the Grecian Valley, it suggests the nature of his relationship with Cobham. Brown is not only apologizing for failing to finish the head of the oval, but protesting against the accusation that he had formed any idea of his own. Clearly Cobham believed his instructions to have been firm. The relationship is exactly what we should have expected from John Penn's account of the sort of gardener Cobham wanted at Stowe — a man who would be 'free from the vanity and conceit which had made his former assistants disinclined to alterations upon which he had determined'.

Furthermore, it is Cobham's instructions that Brown should have followed (or rather denies having been absolutely given), not some plan of Kent's. Altogether the letter strongly supports the argument that Cobham himself was the principal designer of the Grecian Valley. John Penn put the general point even more explicitly: 'Though Lord Cobham zealously patronised him [Brown], he there allowed him no opportunity for substituting any designs of his own'.[29]

But Cobham had also wanted a man who would 'converse instructively on his favourite pursuit' and this implies that he would have listened to, and sometimes been influenced by Brown. It is exactly the sort of relationship which estate owners so often have with their head gardeners, and makes the precise allocation of responsibility for a particular feature impossible. As for Cobham's own ideas, no doubt they were also influenced by those of his friends, relations and fellow gardening enthusiasts. Most notable among these were Alexander Pope and William Pitt, but such relatives as the Grenvilles of Wotton and the Lytteltons of Hagley were also keenly interested. Any one of them could have contributed ideas.

Hussey's claim must finally be justified by the result. Here the argument is finely balanced. On the one hand the valley was an ideal one, aiming to produce garden experiences of the sort that Kent garden features were meant to produce. The Temple of Concord and Victory was its main feature; at the opposite end it was to have reached a climax in a triumphal arch, though this was never built. On the other hand the whole landscaping of the valley with its belts of trees, giving way to lawns which were to sweep down to a small lake, has an unmistakable flavour of Brown, and would have seemed even more characteristic when the solid belts of trees which now enclose it were varied by clumps and shady walks. Brown may not himself have been responsible for this change, but the Grecian Valley was indeed a garden feature of a new kind, a kind in which the landscape itself is most important, a kind which Brown went on to produce again and again.

As for the actual carrying out of the vast project, this took all the next year. 23,500 cubic yards of earth[30] were barrowed away to make a valley out of what had previously been farmland. And the Temple of Concord and Victory was still being built in 1749, the year of Cobham's death.

12. The Queen's Temple at Stowe.

3. On Loan

 THROUGHOUT the 1740s Cobham was generous with his head gardener, lending him to several of his friends and neighbours to help them design their gardens. The first time he did this was during Brown's first ten months at Stowe — further evidence that, from the start, Brown was considered a qualified landscape architect. Ralph Verney told the odd story in a letter dated 31 December 1741:

Mr Soulderns is bit in the sale of his house at Souldern [near Aynho], as are several tradesmen round about. The pretended purchaser... proves to be an attorney's clerk worth nothing and is gone off. He got Lord Cobham's gardener to lay out the gardens, and a master builder was agreed with to new front the house, and treated everybody very handsomely, but with what design nobody knows.[1]

This clerk had also been trying to buy Skeen, and Stoke, but he has never been identified.

From 1742 Cobham may also have occasionally lent Brown to his nephew, Richard Grenville of Wotton, who was later to inherit Stowe,[2] but the story of how Brown returned to Wotton fifteen years later to make one of his most splendid landscapes must be told in its proper place.

Brown was next lent by Cobham to Lord and Lady Denbigh of Newnham Paddox in Warwickshire, five miles north of Rugby. The Denbighs kept a 'Building Book' and on 28 April 1746 this records the start of 'the alterations of the grand canal, and carrying it on to the head of the pond in the park by a plan and the direction of Mr Brown, gardener to Lord Cobham, with other work done in consequence of this'.[3]

Lord Denbigh, the Fifth Earl, and his Countess Isabella had already been improving their gardens for some five years. They were close friends of the Cobhams. In London they were neighbours in Hanover Square. In the country they visited each other. Lady Denbigh, a lively lady, probably inspired the improvements at Newnham Paddox, and Cobham's sister encouraged her, sending

13. Brown's Rotunda at Croome Court, Worcestershire.

her the advice that English elm should be mixed with Dutch elm to make a good hedge quickly.[4] Lord Cobham lent £500.[5] He probably offered Lady Denbigh the loan of Brown during a visit she made to Stowe in the summer of 1745.[6]

Brown continued to work at Newnham Paddox for at least two years. During the winter of 1747-8 the Building Book records the levelling of the end of the serpentine water, the cleaning of the first pond in the park and 'laying it' with hanging slopes on each side.

The Denbighs may then have run short of money, because no new work is recorded till 1753. From November that year, however, till June 1754 they again employed Brown to work on the upper pond. They also commissioned him to rebuild their house. By this time he was well qualified as an architect and had already built Croome Court in Worcestershire for Lord Coventry. At Newnham Paddox work began on pulling down part of the old house in April 1754, so that Brown's new façade could be added.[7]

Next year, however, the Fifth Earl died and was succeeded by Basil, the Sixth Earl. Brown must have found problems in dealing with both the new earl and the countess he soon married. About the latter Lady Craven wrote:

> The Countess of Denbigh was a near neighbour, of whom I stood greatly in awe. I had been informed that Lady Denbigh was a perfect Greek and Latin scholar, and despised the society of the unlearned. Her face and manners were forbidding... either she would not speak at all, or spoke with great *hauteur* to those whom she disliked; and she disliked Lord Craven's wife, and Lord Craven himself, and her own husband, and scarcely deigned to say 'Yes' or 'No' to either of them.[8]

As for Lord Denbigh, he was both nearly deaf and nearly blind. Defending him, his good friend Joseph Cradock said: 'he saw, if objects were placed in a particular light, and he heard, when words were very distinctly articulated'. His infirmities were well known. Fifteen years later when he married his young and pretty second wife, the Queen said to him: 'Denbigh, you have always told me that you was blind; but I am sure you have proved to the contrary, when you made this choice'.[9] One acquaintance described him as a buffoon, but he seems not to have lacked wit. When the King asked him if his wife was a non-juror, he replied that he swore enough for himself and her ladyship likewise.[10] Brown can be imagined standing to the north of the house, where the new work on the ponds was in progress, trying to explain what was happening to the Earl, who could neither hear what he was saying nor see what he was talking about.

From Brown's point of view a still more serious problem was that the Earl was short of money — it seems to have been a family characteristic. The problem was solved when 'an old rich aunt' very kindly gave him '£2,000 to be laid out in the house or gardens. He preferred the latter; for, though the great room, with his fine Vandyke portraits, was built with spaces between the windows to receive the largest glass mirrors from Paris, yet he would prefer completing his large piece of

14. View across one of the lakes at Newnham Paddox, Warwickshire.

water and bridge, which were absolutely necessary for the whole place.'[11]

For the next six years work went steadily ahead at Newnham Paddox and Brown no doubt came regularly to supervise it. The house was finished by 1761 when various workmen were paid the balances due to them.

Mysteries remain about Newnham Paddox. A loose sheet of paper shows that the accounts were not finally wound up until seven years later in 1768, when Brown and others acknowledged final payments. And in September of that year, when Horace Walpole visited Newnham he noted that the new gardens and serpentine water were still being made.[12]

In essence Brown's garden work at Newnham consisted of turning two rectangular ponds of the old formal gardens into two long irregular lakes. From the house the main view was down these, but he brought the larger of them up alongside the house, where before there had been canals and a triangular pond. So much water was thought in Victorian times to make the house damp, and the near end of the big pond was filled. Then in 1870, Brown's house was much expanded in grandiose and tasteless style. All was pulled down in 1952, but the upper lake and a large part of the lower survive. Now that their hanging slopes are being thinned they are recovering a wild charm, even if not exactly what Brown planned.

To return to the 1740s, Cobham probably next lent his head gardener to the Duke of Grafton whose estate at Wakefield lay five miles north-east of Stowe in the Forest of Whittlebury. Here Kent had been rebuilding an old hunting lodge for the duke. Both Kent and Brown are traditionally said to have played a part in designing the grounds, but who did what will never be known since most of the Grafton papers were destroyed earlier this century in a fire.

In front of the house a great lake was created. The work must have been enormous, for the dam is 700 feet long, 25-30 feet wide at the top, some 80 feet wide at the bottom centre and raises the water level 25 feet. Across the lake a 250-acre expanse of parkland, known as Wakefield Lawn was cleared of ancient woodland to rise gently to encircling belts of trees, these broken at intervals to give distant vistas. About the park, Brown-like clumps of trees were dotted. Though the park is now cultivated farmland, its general shape is still clear and the surrounding trees preserved.

There can be little doubt about Brown's role in these various gardens to which Cobham lent him. He would have been no mere head gardener, carrying out the owner's schemes, but giving advice about landscaping and design. There might seem to be a contradiction between the suggestion that Brown was responsible for little of the garden design at Stowe while at the same time he was designing several other gardens, but, given Cobham's age, military background and personal interest in his garden, this seems quite possible. Brown's landscaping in other gardens in the 1740s may indeed explain why garden historians have suggested, without much evidence, that he was at this time the designer of the gardens at Stowe.

Brown's outside work in these years began to give him the confidence he needed to set up as a landscape gardener on his own, but when Cobham died in September 1749 he did not leave Stowe at once. He had personal reasons for staying.

On 24 November 1744 he had married a girl named Bridget Wayet. She came from a 'very respectable county family' of Boston and Tumby in Bain, Lincolnshire.[13] How Brown had met her is not known, but the respectability of her family is a significant indication of the way in which his own status had risen during the five years he had been in the south.

The Browns' wedding took place in the little church of Stowe, a few hundred yards down the slope from the great house. But there was no village here to provide them with a home; its last two houses had been removed in Bridgeman's time. He and his new wife probably lived in the westerly of the two Boycott Pavilions, which face each other like twin pepper-pots across the Oxford Avenue, Stowe's main drive. Certainly this was where Brown's successor at Stowe, Richard Woodward, lived, and it seems probable that he would have taken Brown's house. The pavilions had been built in about 1728, one of them for Major Sam Speed, a fellow soldier of Cobham's, but Speed died before he could occupy it.[14] Their setting diminishes them, and they are in fact the size of lodge cottages; the one which Brown probably occupied now makes two flats.

I. View down the Grecian Valley from the Temple of Concord and Victory at Stowe, Buckinghamshire.

II. (Overleaf) The lake at Newnham Paddox, Warwickshire.

III. Croome Court, Worcestershire, by Richard Wilson.

15. One of the twin Boycott Pavilions at Stowe where Brown and his wife probably lived.

The Browns named their first two children after themselves: Bridget, christened in 1746, and Lancelot, christened in 1748. It is an interesting sidelight on the times, that Bridget must have been conceived when the great Whig landlords of the country were in a panic at the approach of Prince Charles's Scottish army. On 8 December that year (1745) Lord Fermanagh wrote:

> The country was greatly alarm'd on Friday with the rebels... Ld. Cobham pack'd up his arms and plate and the best things and sent them away, but where I don't know. This frightened the people very much. They were carrying his things to Oxford but Mr Greenvill stopt em upon the road and ordered them somewhere else. Ld. Cobham was in town but Mr Dorrel sent to the house and immediately they began to pack up and dismiss the workmen. Twas a simple affair and did hurt as it lower'd people's spirits.[15]

Prince Charles reached Derby, but his bare-footed Highlanders would go no further.

After another two years the Browns had a second son, christened in April 1750, who died before he was a month old. Mrs Brown probably realized that she was pregnant with this child soon after Cobham died and the Browns may well not have considered moving until it had been born.

Another son, John, was born the following year, and again his wife's pregnancy may have played a part in keeping Brown still at Stowe. He may also have been hoping for a job with another landowner of the sort he had had with Cobham and only decided to leave when he got no offer. Perhaps he still felt too inexperienced to risk independence. Certainly he spent the next two years gaining experience. What he had so far done outside Stowe had been interesting, but nothing like as extensive or important as the work he now undertook, in particular at Warwick Castle and Croome Court.

He probably took on these two major projects, which both involved building as well as landscaping, at about the same time, late in 1749. At Warwick Castle he was employed by Francis Lord Brooke, later First Earl of Warwick. The improvement of his property was one of Brooke's main interests and he worked at it throughout his life.

His earliest step was taken in 1744 when he closed two footpaths to the west of the castle used by farmers to drive their animals to the river. Five years later Brown transformed this area, previously consisting of two large parterres, into a lawn, and also planted trees on a narrow strip of river bank close below the castle. In July 1751 Horace Walpole wrote:

> The Castle is enchanting; the view pleased me more than I can express; the River Avon tumbles down a cascade at the foot of it. It is well laid out by one Brown who has set up, on a few ideas of Kent and Mr Southcote. One sees what the prevalence of taste does; little Brook who would have chuckled to have been born in an age of clipped hedges and cockle shell avenues, has submitted to let his garden and park be natural.[16]

In 1753 Brooke signed an agreement with Brown for various alterations to the castle itself. The most curious of these was to extend the family's private apartments near the Great Hall into the castle's massive walls. In 1754 Thomas Gray, the poet, described what had been done, also noting Brooke's small stature (he suffered from a congenital disease). Brooke had now, he wrote: 'a little burrough in the massy walls of the place for his little self and his children, which is hung with paper and printed linen, and carved chimneypieces in the exact manner of Berkley Square or Argyle-Buildings'.[17]

Meanwhile Brown continued to work in the gardens, planting clumps on the island across the river from the castle, a belt of trees round the Temple Meadow beyond, and later (1760) one round Barford Common to the south.

Typically, Brown became a friend of Brooke's. Brooke was one of the distinguished landowners who later supported a petition for Brown to be given a royal gardening appointment. Later again, in 1772, Brooke wrote to Brown asking for a

16. Brown's lawn at Warwick Castle. The mount and Castle can be seen in the background.

reference for a new gardener: 'Lord Warwick's compliments of the season attend his old friend Mr Brown, who he desires to send him a character of John Beecroft, gardener. One is wanted for W. Castle, to take care of the garden, hothouse etc. but particularly an extream sober man.' An earlier one had got so drunk he had fallen downstairs, broken his skull and 'dyed shockingly'. The town of Warwick, Brooke added, was enough to debauch anyone who was not steady and sober by nature.[18]

Brooke's final opinion about Brown's work at Warwick he gave in a letter to Lord Minto of 1766. 'I must say he hitt off the slip of the garden ground well, and it was the first thing he executed after Stowe.'[19]

In the same letter Brooke made a comment on Brown's work in the 1750s which is particularly interesting since it qualifies in an important way the usual idea that he was born a genius. 'I have undone many of the things he left me, as I thought looking formal in the planting way, ever making round clumps that merit nothing but being very tame indeed.' Brown, it seems, was still far from a total convert to naturalness. The sort of clumps which were being created at Warwick are shown in a plan of about 1760. Twenty-one trees in the shape of a filled-in oval are planted with geometric regularity, each tree with the name of a member of the family beside it.[20]

Brown's architectural work at Warwick is not easy to distinguish today. His Gothic porch at the entrance to the hall has been incorporated in a later one. The private rooms of the Brooke family are elaborately set with the waxwork figures of a late Victorian week-end. Outside, his raised courtyard cannot be missed; and the cedars he planted, now mature trees, stand among many other native and exotic species on the great sweep of lawn to the west of the castle mound. The narrow piece of land between the castle and the river, however, is again treeless, and across the river Brown's plantings have been swamped by later ones.

At Croome Court, seven miles south of Worcester, Brown's landscaping was more extensive. So, too, was his architectural work. It is an astonishing tribute to the trust he could inspire that already, although he was quite unproved as an architect, he should have been given an entire great country mansion to design and build. His employer here was the Sixth Earl of Coventry, who had inherited from his brother a low-lying, marshy estate between the rivers Severn and Avon. Horace Walpole called Coventry 'a grave young lord of the remains of the Patriot breed'.[21] This comment, usually quoted out of context, referred to Coventry's marriage to Maria Gunning, the elder of the two Gunning sisters. According to Walpole, Coventry had been infatuated with Maria for a year, but had only summoned up the courage to marry her when the Duke of Hamilton had been so besotted with Elizabeth, Maria's younger sister, that he had married her at midnight, using, in default of a wedding ring, one from his bed curtains.[22] The remarkable thing about the Gunning sisters, Walpole wrote, was not so much that either was outstandingly beautiful as that both were so equally beautiful.[23]

Perhaps Lady Coventry found her husband dull. He was a keen sportsman, excusing himself in August 1745 from visiting a friend because 'September and October I always dedicate to Diana the Huntress and that with so obstinate a zeal that no allurement' could drag him away.[24] And he had a limited appetite for the society of guests. As well as a new great house, he wanted a lodge, explaining that 'the hospitality my ancestors exercised for some generations at Croomb makes it impossible for me to effect any privacy or retirement there. It has always been an inn and always must remain so.'[25] Whatever the reason, his wife began a notorious affair with the Duke of Bolingbroke, which was later to have a curious effect on another of Brown's commissions (see page 78).

Despite his personal problems, Coventry was considered a local benefactor. For fifty-eight years he was Lord Lieutenant of Worcestershire. When he died (many years after Brown, in 1809), Judge Perrot wrote that he 'might be truly said to have brought millions into the county' by building, road-making and encouraging 'useful public institutions'.[26] On his own house and grounds alone he was said to have spent the vast sum of £400,000.[27]

Coventry may have been persuaded to employ Brown by his friend, the now forgotten architect, Sanderson Miller. In 1752 Coventry wrote to Miller to tell him that 'whatever merits it [Croome] may in future time boast it will be ungrateful not to acknowledge you the primary author... nothing can be more kind than your congratulations on the subject of the bedchamber'. It had been Miller who had shown him that 'Nature had been more liberal to me than I apprehended'.[28] Miller knew Brown and had taken long walks with him at Stowe, during which he probably discussed Croome's problems with Brown and offered to recommend him to Coventry.[29]

The chief of these problems was water. The old house stood on ground so marshy that Brown had to create an extensive drainage system before he could begin the new one. Then he built a Palladian mansion, using Bath stone. Visitors were impressed. In August 1750 Lord Guernsey was 'glad of [Miller's] surprise at what [Coventry] has done at Croome, as I wish him success in his undertaking'.[30] In November the next year Sir Edward Turner reported that Lord Coventry was 'furnishing his house with elegance. He complains of its amplitude.'[31] On the whole Coventry was delighted. In the same letter to Miller he wrote that 'Mr Brown has done very well by me, and indeed I think has studied both my place and my pocket, which are not always conjunctively the objects of prospectors'.

17. Croome Court, Worcestershire, Brown's first major architectural work.

In the grounds Brown used the surplus water to form a lake and a new winding river. He included in his design a Corinthian summerhouse on an island, a grotto and a rotunda. Some years passed before, in 1758, Brown came back to Croome to design and build a Gothic church. A delightful painting of about this date by Richard Wilson shows Brown's river, the house in sunlight, and the tower of the new church on the hilltop beyond.[32]

Water continued to cause Coventry problems. The lake began to leak and in November 1772 he wrote to ask Brown to 'send me a man of practice and sound direction for that important work. I call it so, because all the enjoyment of Croome next summer will depend on it... Cou'd Mr Read be spar'd? As he first made the head [the dam] he wou'd be the fittest person to restore it. I believe the roots of the trees have been a chief cause of the fissures in the bank.'[33]

Coventry acknowledged that at Croome Court Brown had been the chief architect of his achievements by erecting a monument to him beside the lake, with an inscription reading:

> To the Memory of
> Lancelot Brown
> who by the powers of
> his inimitable
> and creative genius
> formed this garden scene
> out of a morass.

Brown worked for Coventry longer than for any other client and they, too, became good friends. It was with Coventry that Brown had been dining in London on the night of his death many years later.

The skeleton of Brown's work at Croome survives. For about thirty years after the Second World War the house, with its twin square towers and odd row of arched chimneys, was the property of the International Society for Krishna Consciousness. Thereafter it stood, solid but somewhat derelict, waiting for a new owner, in an expanse of bare ground. During recent droughts Brown's river became a bed of bulrushes. Today the little summerhouse temple on the island is surrounded by a wilderness of brambles and the head of the lake is again leaking. But in 1983 the monument to Brown was re-erected by the lakeside to celebrate the two hundredth anniversary of his death, and there is charm in its semi-abandoned surroundings, with their ancient trees, some of which are certainly Brown's, even if nature at Croome is again much in need of Brown's attention to correct its 'accidents'.

Just how keenly Brown was looking for freelance work during the two years he stayed at Stowe after Cobham's death is shown by a letter he wrote in October 1750 to George Bowes of Gibside, Durham. Bowes wanted to build a monumental column. To prove how well qualified he was for the job, Brown gave details of the dimensions of the Cobham memorial he had recently built at Stowe. He asked for a

18. Brown's Gothic church at Croome Court.

sketch of what Bowes wanted, and for the weight of a cubic foot of the local stone. 'The scaffolding of buildings of this kind is the greatest arte in the whole, after the foundations,' he wrote. 'The wind has a very great effect on buildings that stands on so small a base and should be well attended to... I should have a double pleasure in [building] it your situation being my native country.'[34]

The monument was never built, but within a few months Brown had made up his mind to leave Stowe and set up on his own.

4. His Own Man

IT IS EASY, as it is with William Kent, to describe the sort of gardens which Brown now began to design in increasing numbers in every part of England except the far south-west. He created lakes or winding rivers with lawns running down to them, these set with clumps of trees, the whole surrounded by an enclosing belt of trees. The tree clumps were of different species, to give contrasts of colour at different times of the year, and placed to allow a variety of views between them. The lawns undulated to provide contrasts of light and shade at different seasons and times of day. The surrounding belt of trees was broken to give views of the countryside beyond. The lakes and rivers flowed out, or into each other over rocky cascades, and the lakes were contrived to end with bridges or pass out of sight so that they seemed to be rivers. Above all, the house became important in the garden. The garden was to be viewed from the house, and the house was also to be the garden's chief feature. It was to be viewed in particular from approaching carriageways, and from points along carriageways which ran inside the encircling belt of trees.

This may be one of the reasons why Brown continued to design houses as well as gardens. That was certainly the opinion of the poet and gardener, the Revd William Mason. 'Brown,' he wrote, '... was ridiculed for turning architect, but I have always thought he did it from a kind of necessity having found the great difficulty which must frequently have occurred to him in forming a picturesque whole, where the previous building had been ill-placed, or of improper dimensions.'[1]

But as with Kent, the purpose behind Brown's landscapes is more obscure because it depended on a philosophy to which we no longer subscribe. He and his contemporaries were idealists, in the Aristotelean sense. They believed that nature was always tending towards the ideal, but failing to reach it because of accidents. The landscape gardener's duty was to eliminate these accidents.

For the next thirty-two years Brown's style and the purpose behind it varied only a little. The surprising thing is not that after twenty years it was violently attacked — by the architect Sir William Chambers and his supporters — but that Brown

19. The interior of Brown's Rotunda at Petworth, West Sussex.

and his work remained the height of fashion for so long.

It was to Hammersmith, then a small riverside village, that Brown moved from Stowe in the autumn of 1751, to set up the private practice which was to transform, directly or by its influence, all but a very few of England's great gardens, not to mention thousands of smaller ones. Here he settled in a house in Hammersmith Mall, with his wife and four children, Bridget, now five years old, Lancelot, John and Margaret. Margaret had been christened earlier that year at Stowe. Why he chose Hammersmith we don't know. Certainly there were nursery gardens there, those of Kennedy and Lee for example, which he later patronized, and in due course he became much involved with the Holland family — Henry Holland the builder, and his son Henry Holland, the architect — who lived nearby in Fulham. But it is merely a guess that either of these explains his choice.

For the next thirteen years he worked here on an increasing number of projects. Here, judging by their quantity, he must often have sat up late at night, drawing plans, compiling his accounts and writing letters. From here he set out on his many expeditions to inspect the progress of his works. Here, too, he must have been nursed during his recurring illnesses, which were probably attacks of asthma but may have been bronciectasis, and were certainly exacerbated by long days in unheated carriages and nights in the cold bedrooms of inns or great houses.

In the autumn of 1751 he was already at work on Croome Court, Warwick Castle and another Warwickshire garden, Packington. During the next four years, apart from returning to rebuild and continue landscaping Newnham Paddox for the Denbighs, he took on at least six new major projects, the last of which, Burghley, was to need him for twenty-five years.

One of the first and most interesting was for Sir James Dashwood at Kirtlington, ten miles north of Oxford in the Cherwell valley, partly for what Brown did here, but also because it shows that he had no special bias towards Whig clients and would work for whoever wanted him. Sir James was one of the most influential of the old Tory landowners of Oxfordshire. His new house, built between 1742 and 1746 by John Sanderson, was considered the finest in the county after Blenheim. He could ride on his own land from Kirtlington to Banbury, a distance of some fourteen miles, and had been a Member of Parliament for the county since 1740.[2]

He was a man of formidable build. At the age of thirty-five he weighed 17 stone.[3] He would weigh himself in competition with a Mr Sheldon, the only man in the county who could compete with him.[4] Sheldon was just one of his Roman Catholic friends, and he was suspected of Jacobite sympathies.

Sir James was probably better known in his time than his cousin, Sir Francis Dashwood of the Hell Fire Club, particularly after the notorious Oxfordshire election, in which he was one of the defeated Tory candidates. The campaign opened in 1752 with a great fete at Kirtlington, and before the poll in April 1754 Dashwood had spent £5,736 5s 7d in bribing and entertaining the voters.[5] It was precisely in these years, and during the following one when Parliament was

20. Kirtlington, Oxfordshire, across the lake.

questioning the result, that Brown was working for him.

Why he turned to Brown is not known, but Sanderson Miller may have recommended him, as he probably had to Lord Coventry at Croome, and almost certainly soon did to Lord Dacre at Belhus.

When Brown first came to Kirtlington he found an estate of much interest but one which presented him with problems. The first of these was topographical. Though Dashwood's new house stood on a useful hill, the land in front of it stretched away without rise or fall till it reached the Chilterns thirty miles to the south. All about this wide flat landscape stood fine oaks, some the ancient trees of the Great Wood, others forming the New Wood, correctly a plantation, indeed perhaps the earliest of all English plantations,[6] ordered by the Duke of Clarence in 1476.[7] Both woods were probably being managed as wood-pasture, and the trees would have stood on well grazed grassland.

Brown's second problem was that Dashwood had already obtained a plan for his estate from the royal gardener, Thomas Greening. It shows the house thickly surrounded by woodland — either the existing woods or proposed new plantations — among which paths run to various temples. This woodland cut off all view from the house to the south-west and south-east.

Though Greening's plan has written on it, 'totally changed by Browne,' in fact Brown left these woods or plantations, and, judging by the age of today's trees,

21. View from the house to the grounds at Kirtlington.

even added to them, in particular using yew. He did, however, eliminate most of their paths and garden monuments.

Beyond them, in the outer park his design was more typical. Here his plan shows small clumps, brief avenues and single trees (the only large clump has been scratched through, as if he or Dashwood decided against it), then in the middle distance a lake. The lake and many of these trees survive.

It may seem surprising that Brown sited this lake so far away, where it usually appears as no more than a thin bright line. It is fed by no stream, and there is flat land much closer to the house. Here, on the other hand, it makes an important contribution to the sense of Kirtlington's vastness. To suggest that he should have put it closer is to require him in retrospect to have done precisely what his detractors most often complain about: made yet another garden to a single formula.

The present owner, with the intention of producing a more Brown-like effect, is thinning the large woods and plantations to the south-east and south-west of the house, though preserving some of the magnificent trees which Brown planted. To the north, exceptionally fine oaks still stand in parkland. They are probably of the same date and certainly not those of the Duke of Clarence's plantation. The most spectacular view, however, is now, as it must always have been, *from* the lake. The house then appears on its distant hilltop, flanked by trees, silhouetted against the northern sky.

Brown began to work for the Second Earl of Egremont at Petworth in Sussex at about the same time that he first worked for Sir James Dashwood. There is less doubt about who recommended him. Egremont's sister, Elizabeth, was the wife of George Grenville. It was George Grenville, the future Prime Minister, who had taken over Wotton in Buckinghamshire now that his brother Richard, later Earl Temple, had succeeded Cobham at Stowe. Brown had, in fact, been consulted about Petworth before he left Stowe, for there are records in the Petworth archives of payments to him for journeys from Stowe.

The gardens at Petworth are among the most splendid of Brown's early creations. They are of special interest, for here he not only landscaped a great park but alongside it embellished a small pleasure garden in an earlier mode.

Egremont had inherited Petworth in 1740 when he was thirty years old, been on the grand tour where he became an enthusiastic collector of Old Masters, and then turned to politics. He was described by Horace Walpole as 'a composition of pride, ill nature, avarice and strict good-breeding; with such infamy in his frame that he could not speak the truth on the most trivial occasions'.[8] But Brown's dealings with him provide little evidence to support Walpole. Later Egremont was Ambassador to the Congress of Augsburg. He found this a trying appointment, remarking in 1761 that if he survived his next three turtle dinners he would become immortal.[9] He died in 1763 and as a result enjoyed Brown's finished work at Petworth for only about two years.

Egremont's first serious move (1751) was to have a plan prepared of his grounds as they then existed.[10] Close to the south and east of the house lay the small town of Petworth and this left only areas to the west and north to garden. To the west came first a walled rectangle, created probably by those once fashionable gardeners in the formal French style, George London and Henry Wise. A painting of about 1700[11] shows this as even more starkly formal than most gardens of the period. Beyond its iron railings and gate a wide avenue led across marshy ground and ponds, passing the point at which a vast stable block had stood till 1725. Formal terraces, called ramparts, rose above this area to the north. To the north of the house itself, beyond a parterre and an orangery, lay the Pleasure Ground, described as the Wilderness, a comparatively small hilly area criss-crossed by a geometrical pattern of paths, these called birchen walks, but probably lined with cypresses.

The following year Brown drew his own plan, and in each of the next four years (1753-56) he signed a contract with Egremont for different phases of the work.[12] The sixth item of the first contract describes the feature which was to transform Petworth: 'To now make the Horse Pond in all its parts'. The Horse Pond, so called because it was in the little valley beyond the old stables, became the lake which now lies at the centre of the view from the house. Between the lake and the house Brown made the old rectangular walled garden into a vast lawn, while to the north he reduced the terraces to 'fine undulating steps adorned with Groupes of Cedars, Pines etc'. At the summit of the ridge above the terraces, as well as beyond

22. Brown's expanded 'Horse Pond' which is now the lake at the centre of the view from Petworth House.

the lake, he left ancient timber standing or planted new trees. These, many of them Spanish chestnut, are the magnificent veterans of today. Ridge and high ground enclose the park to the north and west. To the south it is ringed more distantly by the Sussex Downs.

Though Brown had now made a number of lakes, the making of Petworth's caused problems, and in the contract of June 1755 he undertook 'The alteration of the pond in all its parts (viz.) the digging all such parts out as are not deep enough, according to the stakes. The making all the necessary clay walls. The levelling the bottom and making the slopes and for pitching the sides being 2460 feet and upwards to prevent the cattle from damaging it...'[13]

This description gives Brown's dam for the lake at Petworth special interest. A few years earlier another 'landscape engineer', John Grundy, had begun designing

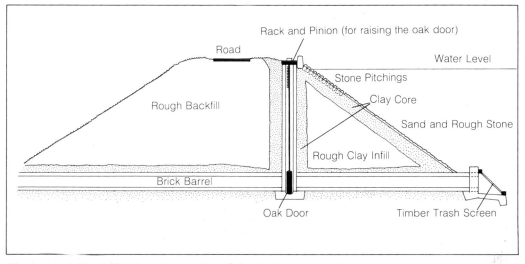

23. Petworth Pond Head: an impression of the dam's construction.

dams with vertical central walls of clay. In 1749 Grundy drew a cross-section of such a dam in a proposal for a lake at Grimsthorpe, Lincolnshire, for the Duke of Ancaster. Grundy is generally considered to have been the first to design and build earth dams of this sort. Dams to the same design were still being built in the 1960s.[14]

It is an odd fact that Brown, in none of his many contracts or plans, ever included cross-sectional drawings of his dams. But recent investigations at Petworth have confirmed what the words of the 1755 contract suggest, that the dam has just such a central clay wall. Brown later worked at Grimsthorpe and probably met Grundy then. Possibly he already knew him in the 1750s. If not, within seven years of Grundy's design for Grimsthorpe, Brown had on his own designed a dam of a very similar kind and was building it at Petworth.

The dam included an arrangement for draining the lake. This consisted of a well-like structure of brick, set at the centre of the vertical clay wall. Down this well a pole could be inserted to raise or lower a wooden door, so opening or shutting a horizontal drainage tunnel which ran below the dam. At the inner end of this drainage tunnel below the water there was a screen to prevent it being blocked with trash.

The pitching mentioned in the contract was of stone and faced the sloping inner side of the dam at water level. The lower part of this slope was protected with rougher stone and sand. Beneath these top layers the whole of the inner slope of the dam consisted of another layer of clay. Ordinary soil, mixed with a certain amount of clay formed the rest of the dam.

Three months later Egremont seems to have been questioning Brown's charges, for Brown wrote (12 August 1755):

I came home last Saturday much out of order, having had a return of my old complaint. I continue to have an extreme bad cough... [I will examine again] the article of the pond... as soon as I am able to... but my head at this time is very unfit for employments of that kind... Your Lordship will find that the clay walls are far from being finished... there is a vast deal of earth to be moved or else your Lordship will have nothing but weeds and dirty water.[15]

If, as seems likely, he was here referring to the layer of clay below the pitching, this was apparently not part of the original design, but was being added because the lake had given trouble.

Troubles, however, continued. A year later (28 July 1756) Brown received 'a disagreeable letter' from Blair, the Petworth steward, telling him that the water level was falling. 'I am doubtful the springs have abatted,' he wrote, 'if that should be the case the sinking is the less to be wondered at, however if there are faults they shall be mended.' Once again Brown had been ill and excused himself for failing to come to Petworth. While he was writing this letter he was interrupted. 'The doctor has been with me this moment and tells me if I do not immediately go to the sea and bathe he is very sure that my fever and cough will return again.'[16]

But Egremont can hardly have doubted that the lake would ultimately be satisfactory for in the same year he had already contracted with Brown to build a second. This lay beyond the ridge, in the northern park, and became the central feature of another vast but more enclosed bowl of countryside.

The four hundred fallow deer which still mainly live here can spread over the ridge into the area of the main lake, indeed right up to the windows of the house, for the lawn has no ha-ha. Brown did, however, protect the Pleasure Ground with one. Into this smaller hilly area he introduced a Doric temple, moved from the terraces, and an Ionic rotunda, possibly to his own design. They survive — though the rotunda has lost its roof — well sited on high points. So do a large number of fine trees, many of them again Spanish chestnut, which Brown planted. But the area is today somewhat overgrown and it is hard to make out the serpentine paths Brown introduced, one of which was to run 'on through the laurels leading up to the seat where the Duchess of Somerset [Egremont's aunt] used to drink her coffee'.[17]

Along the paths Brown agreed to plant not only laurels but flowers and shrubs. A number of records of the types of trees which Brown ordered from nurseries have survived, but virtually none of the shrubs and flowers. Petworth is an exception. In 1753 he received a bill from the nurseryman John Williams for twenty-nine species.[18] Enthusiastic plantsmen have used this list as evidence that Brown was a plantsman too, just as interested in the colours and details of his grand designs as in their total effect. But though the list includes roses, butcher's broom, honeysuckle, jasmine, trumpet flowers and other shrubs and flowers, it also includes many trees — ilex, bird cherry, double cherry, double thorn, Virginian Sumach, American Maple, laburnum and acacia. And the fact that it is the only such list to have

IV. Brown's Rotunda amidst trees at Petworth, West Sussex.

V. Petworth House.

VI. The Lion Bridge at Burghley, Northamptonshire.

VII. Brown's Orangery at Burghley House.

24. Brown's Doric Temple at Petworth.

been found argues more persuasively that he was *not* usually concerned with shrub or flower details.

Egremont was well enough pleased with Brown's work at Petworth to be one of the fourteen estate owners who signed the same petition to the Duke of Newcastle in 1758 to 'promote his speedy appointment to the care of Kensington Gardens', but he died before Brown obtained any such royal appointment.

While Brown was signing contracts with Egremont at Petworth he was taking on other new work, in particular at Beechwood for Sir John Sebright, and at Moor Park for Admiral Anson, both in Hertfordshire. It was Egremont who had recommended him to Anson.[19]

Though Moor Park is now a well known golf club and outlying parts of its grounds have been built on, the essence of Brown's landscaping is still easy to see. Here, too, he made a pleasure garden, but oddly enough set its small lake up above the house and out of sight. Elsewhere the last but one owner, Benjamin Sykes, had spent £5,000 of his gains from selling his shares in the notorious South Sea Company at their high point (when the £1 shares were worth £1,200) on removing a hill in front of the house.[20] Brown now attempted to vary the flatness of the ground with a number of artificial hills. Horace Walpole was unimpressed. 'I was not struck with it,' he wrote in 1760, 'after all the miracles I had heard that Brown had performed there. He has undulated the horizon in so many artificial mole-hills that it is full as unnatural as if it was drawn with a rule and compasses. Nothing is done to the house; there are not even chairs in the great apartment. My Lord Anson is more slatternly than the Churchills...'[21] Moor Park's Temple of the Winds which stood in the pleasure garden beside the lake was destroyed by a falling tree in this century.[22] The undulations of its grounds seem if anything more mole-hill-like, now that they are set about with shaven greens and fairways.

Anson had experienced trouble getting Brown's attention when he first wrote to him in September 1753, saying that he was sorry to hear of Brown's indisposition.[23] This was an earlier illness than those Brown described in letters to Egremont and continued until October, when a more interesting client was trying to engage him. It was then that Thomas Lennard Barrett (Lord Dacre, as he became) wrote to his close friend Sanderson Miller: 'Brown has been here and by what I find has really been very ill'.[24] Like many valetudinarians, Dacre had apparently been too preoccupied with his own ill health to find it easy to believe in someone else's.

Self-concerned, anxious and timid as he was, Dacre seems to have been an agreeable person, a great admirer of Miller's Gothic designs — and a sympathizer when Miller's new steeple at Wroxton Abbey fell down. He was said to look strikingly like Charles I, no doubt because his grandmother, the Countess of Sussex, was the illegitimate daughter of Charles II. His father had died before he was born and his paternal grandfather had removed him from the care of Lady Anne, his mother, in case she brought him up a Papist.[25] His letters to Miller are full of references to his depressions. In May 1745 he wrote: 'The cold Bath which I have gone into for three weeks past has quite recovered my weak nerves and restored me to good Spirits and the Blew Devils are quite gone away, not, I suppose, very well relishing cold water'.[26] That autumn he asked Miller to get him a new horse or he would die for want of exercise. 'You know I am a great coward o'horseback and a very bad rider, the first the result of the last. So the horse must be absolutely very sure footed and very quiet... he must not start nor stumble, that's poz... don't get me a prancing horse which is such a one as I know you love.'[27] Twelve years later he explained to Miller how to avoid depressions:

Bustle then bustle when the Blew Devils make their onset. The best way is to fly them and plunge into society: eat wholesome meats; few flabby or flatulent ones: or that produce bile; as butter, pye crust, etc., etc., your favourites; drink not much tea; or coffee, or even chocolate but with moderation. Let no one thing induce you to read too serious or abstracted books: Don Quixote is better for you than all of them put together... Ride frequently a good round trott: and walk moderately and *take care of standing still when you are warm to talk or look at your labourers.* Get up early in the morning and never lie and doze though you have had a bad night. Drink every day a sup of wine at dinner or after. There are certain camphire pills which Dr. Akenside prescribed me last autumn from which (when much agitated) I have found infinite relief.[28]

Dacre had inherited his Essex property of Belhus in 1745 when he was twenty-eight, and by January 1748 had begun major improvements which included the ploughing of 60 acres for a lawn and widening his river.[29] But when, the next year, his much loved child, Barbara, died, he had gone abroad. Brown's visit of 1753 is the first evidence that he had recovered his enthusiasm for improving his grounds at Belhus. The letter gives a vivid picture of Brown at work and suggests how he would compensate for his lateness by much industry and cheerful enthusiasm: 'he made me a great many very serious professions how ready he was to serve me and while he stayed here slaved at setting out the road and the rest of the Shrubbery all day and drew plans all evening and was in the best humour possible; and of his own accord promised to come again next month. Upon the whole I begin now to think that he has not grown too great to despise my little businesses.'[30]

From this time landscaping under Brown's direction continued at Belhus for three or four years. He was there in 1756, to discuss some plantations. And in January 1759, when Dacre had a new surge of enthusiasm, he again sent for Brown. He wrote to Miller:

In the state I am in, you will perhaps think me bold to begin such a great work as I am going to mention to you... In a word then, I have had Brown down with me at Belhouse and am going to make a pool where now the run of water is, in the lower part of my park: its size will be about 10 acres; its form very irregular and 'twill be a quarter mile long. Brown and indeed my own little judgment tells me that it will be a very great ornament to that side of the park and quite change the face of it.[31]

But the 10 acre lake was not made, for in 1761 he wrote again to Miller: 'I have a number of expenses on me this year and yet I doubt whether I shall have prudence enough to abstain from meddling with my water in the lower part of the park; ...I know that that coarse meadow and moory sided canal might be converted into a very pleasing scene: And Brown is of the same opinion: we now have another scheme; it is to make it in the river stile instead of the lake.'[32]

From this time onwards information is scarce. Another gardener, Richard Woods of Essex, an exact contemporary of Brown's, worked at Belhus. At least another three times (at Harewood, Wardour and Wynnstay) Brown and Woods were again to work on the same gardens, and Woods eventually came to feel that he was undervalued and underpaid in comparison with Brown (see page 164). Here at Belhus he received a total of £250 in 1771.[33] Precisely what he did is uncertain but he may well have been responsible for the final form of the Long Pond, into which the Running Water Brook was eventually transformed.[34] It was to Brown, however, that Dacre still instinctively turned. On 7 November 1773 he was much disappointed that another illness had prevented Brown coming. He assured Brown that he would not move a step without his advice, and asked Brown to call on him when he came to London.[35]

Belhus has gone, pulled down in 1957 after being hit by a bomb in the last war[36] but the first few courses of its brick walls survive among the greens and fairways of a borough council golf course. The M25 sweeps up one side of the park, cutting off the Long Pond's head and island from its tail. But there is enough here to show that Dacre's principal problem in making a dramatic landscape was that his park was almost perfectly flat. And among a great many younger trees there is a fine old clump of London Planes which could well be Brown's. Apart from the problems of the site, it seems probable that Dacre was too susceptible to alternating moods of pessimism and euphoria for Belhus ever to have become one of Brown's great parks. Just the same, his long connection with Dacre is of much interest, showing him both at his most elusive, and for one moment, at his most charming and obliging.

The year after he first went to Belhus Brown was consulted about Burghley, the Cecil palace just outside Stamford on the Northamptonshire-Lincolnshire borders. A quarter of a century later, when staying at Burghley, Brown wrote to another client: 'This is a great place, where I have had twenty-five years pleasure in restoring the monument of a great minister to a great queen'.[37]

The great minister had been Lord Burghley, Queen Elizabeth's Lord Treasurer, who had begun his palatial house in 1552, taking his title from its site — Burghe Minster had once stood here. Some hundred and sixty years later Daniel Defoe described it as 'more like a town than a house...; the towers and the pinnacles so high, and placed at such distances from one another, look like so many distant parish churches'.[38]

By this time George London had been employed to give it formal gardens. There were trimmed avenues, Dutch canals and basins, a wilderness or maze and, in earlier style, vineyards and a mount.

None of this had changed when, in 1754, Brownlow Cecil, Ninth Earl of Exeter, inherited Burghley. He was twenty-nine years old, and an energetic young man who enjoyed foreign travel. Robert Owen, the socialist industrial reformer, who was an apprentice at Stamford, remembered meeting the Earl walking in the park at Burghley alone at night, when neither of them could sleep.[39] The Revd William Cole, who visited Burghley in 1763 with Horace Walpole, called him 'a man of good plain understanding'. He was childless but 'had lately taken home to him a son of his brother, who married a Columbine belonging to the playhouse at Brussels'. More important to Brown, when the Earl's wife, Letitia Townshend, died in 1756 she left her husband £70,000 (for his life only) and so enabled him to continue the improvements to his house and garden which he had begun.[40]

Of the two, the Earl put his house first, and it was in this order that the work was done. At once he commissioned from a York surveyor, John Haynes, plans of the house and gardens as they existed and gave these to Brown as a basis from which to work. In return Brown submitted plans with suggested changes. For many years Brown's plans were lost until, in the 1970s, Dr Eric Till found them at Burghley, in a folder among some 'wishy-washy Victorian water colours' in an electricity meter cupboard.

Brown was soon (May 1756) discussing his plans for Burghley with his old friend Dacre, telling him that he intended to retain whatever was 'Gothick' in the house, for example in the old hall. If Dacre can be trusted, Brown also admired Sanderson Miller's Gothic work and was anxious to show Miller what he intended, but excused himself from sending his drawings because they were 'so large it was impossible'.[41] His main plan indeed measures 5 ft by 3 ft.

Brown's most important suggestion was to raise the walls to make the whole

25. Burghley House, Northamptonshire.

length of the southern facade between the two corner towers a more even height. The result has been to give this front an imposing unity, even though it is in a sense a fake one. All the second-floor windows were anyway false, to allow for the height of the first-floor state rooms. Behind their top sections, which Brown now added, there is nothing at all.

The work began the same year and included removing the house's north-western wing to open a view in that direction, but this was probably the Earl's idea, not Brown's. Brown's plan shows a new library in this wing, with a large new bow window. Throughout his work at Burghley, in particular his alterations to the house, he was probably made to conform closely to the Earl's ideas of what should be done. The 1815 guide to Burghley says about the Earl: 'When few were better qualified to adorn a court, or manage the affairs of state, he preferred retirement at his country seat'. Here he was 'a principal contributor' towards its beautifying and furnishing. He 'had a great genius for painting and architecture, and a superior judgement in both, as every part of this noble structure will testify.'[42] Brown knew how to handle a client of this sort. For eight years he had worked at Stowe for Cobham, another childless employer who had taken a professional interest in everything that was done and had had a mind of his own.

The rebuilding continued throughout the 1760s. The Earl showed Cole and Walpole 'several rooms of paintings which were not hung up... but designed for other rooms when they were completed', and the 'Noble old hall' was still to be modernized.[43]

Work on the gardens followed during the 1770s, but no Brown plan for them has been found. Like so many garden plans, it was probably used on site in all weathers and ultimately fell to pieces. But the estate account books, and the gardens as they survive show what was done.

Brown's new lake dominates. It stretches for a mile, beginning to the west of the house, reaching across its whole southern front, then circling to the east. The start of the work is marked by the purchase in 1775 of twenty-four wheelbarrows, and by payments to a contractor for dredging an old pond which the new lake was to include.[44]

For most of its length the ground rises effectively though not dramatically on both sides to contain the water, and only at its eastern end did Brown have to build an embankment and a dam. The lake has another peculiarity. If Brown had extended it a further 20 yards at its head he would have reached a large geological fault and all would have drained away. He probably knew of this danger, for the Haynes plan of 1755 shows a 'swallow pit' just to the north, so his design was a daring one. In carrying it out he had difficulties. A walk in the shrubbery was 'lower by many feet, than the surface of this noble stream; and twice or thrice, when the workmen thought it well secured, did it elude their pains, surmount its dam, and carrying all before it, subject them to new toil'.[45]

Over the centuries Brown's lake at Burghley has continued to give trouble, with the result that, as at Petworth, we now know precisely how it was made. Surprisingly, here at Burghley, working in limestone country where lakes are notoriously difficult, he seems to have abandoned his earlier vertical-clay-wall design and relied only on a layer of clay below the stone pitching.

It is not the dam itself, however, which has caused Burghley's problems, but the arrangements for draining the lake. As at Petworth, there is a vertical well at the dam's centre, giving access to a drainage tunnel below the dam. But at Burghley this is closed not by an oak door but by a conical wooden plug. The inside end of the drainage tunnel is closed with another wooden plug which must be 'fished for' from a boat when it is to be removed. At least three times — before the First World War, in the 1950s and most recently in 1984 — the plugs have rotted and the resulting rush of water has severely damaged the dam.

Brown also built a large stable block around a courtyard, a Gothic orangery and a fine stone bridge which crosses the lake at its western end. It is know as the Lion Bridge, after the four lions couchant which he placed on its parapets. And as usual he swept away flowerbeds, setting the house in wide lawns which sloped down to the lake, built a ha-ha to keep out the deer and cattle, and moved large amounts of earth to create an artificial hill beside the lake. He also planted trees and 'removed trees of the most enormous bulk, from place to place, to suit the prospect and landscape',[46] doubtless using the sort of machine he had invented at Stowe.

Something strange happened in 1778 or 1779. For twenty-five years the Earl and Brown had been on friendly terms. The Earl had been one more of the fourteen landowners who had supported the petition to the Duke of Newcastle to have

Brown given a royal gardening appointment. In letters to Brown he would end, 'May happy new years ever attend the family at Hampton [where Brown had moved] is the sincere wish of yours, Exeter'.[47] He had made numerous payments to Brown in the 1750s and 1760s[48] and from 1770 to 1777 paid him a regular £1000 a year in six-monthly instalments.[49] In 1778 these ceased, and in 1779 the Burghley steward wrote after a final payment of £214 5s 5d, 'being in full of his account', a clear indication that this was a last settlement.[50] Yet the lake was not finally filled till 1784. What happened we shall probably never know.

Brown's departure from the Burghley payroll is one reason for thinking that the fine, stone, double staircase leading up into Verrio's 'Hell Room' was not designed by him. Certainly he submitted plans for a staircase here in 1781 and 1782, and claimed that he was due payment for them,[51] but the work had already begun and the dimensions of the staircase as it was built correspond closely to those of a design by Adam.[52]

In quite a different way, however, Brown's influence continued at Burghley. Although the small temple, now set among Brown's mature cedars where it looks down from Brown's artificial hill onto his lake, was not built till four years after his death, its plan was his.

Ten years later — 1797 — the historian of Burghley wrote that 'It was the genius of the late LAUNCELOT BROWN which, brooding over the shapeless mass, educed out of a seeming wilderness, all the order and delicious harmony which now prevail'. He picked out in particular the view from the Lion Bridge which commanded 'a very general prospect of the towering mansion, the herds of deer, droves of cattle, and flocks of Spanish sheep'.[53] Though the deer are now elsewhere, it remains the finest view of Burghley. At that time Brown's portrait by Nathaniel Dance[54] hung in the temple. Now it is in Burghley's Pagoda room.

In 1755 when Brown, aged thirty-eight, had taken on the rebuilding and landscaping of Burghley for the Earl of Exeter, he could hardly have realized that this job would last most of the rest of his life. On the other hand by then he must have felt well pleased with the way his plan to establish himself as an independent landscape gardener and architect was succeeding. He had worked by now not only on ten or a dozen major houses and gardens, but was well known to an even larger number of peers of the realm or landed gentlemen. He could afford — or potential clients like Dacre believed that he could afford — to choose what work he took, and reject as unworthy of him their 'little businesses'. He had started a bank account with Hoare's Bank in October 1752, closed it six months later, then in July 1753 started another by depositing £200 with Drummonds Bank.[55] This he was to keep for the rest of his life, during which time some £100,000 passed through it. Most important of all, he must by now have felt confirmed in his belief that he had the technical skill to give his employers what they wanted, and the manner, half familiar-friend, half respectful-servant, to inspire their confidence. At home in Hammersmith his family had increased by one when his final child, Thomas, was born. By now Bridget, his oldest, was nine.

5. Fame

BROWN'S BEST KNOWN CLIENT in the following year, 1756, was the actor David Garrick. The job was a small one. Garrick had built a temple by the side of the Thames at Hampton where it was separated from his house by a road, and Brown suggested that this should be crossed by a tunnel rather than a bridge. When Garrick told Dr Johnson about the tunnel he made one of his more laboured comments: 'David, David, what can't be over-done, may be under-done'.[1] But Brown and his style were now sufficiently in Garrick's mind for him in 1757 to amend his play, *Lethe or Aesop in the Shades*, to include the following comment on the river Styx.

> Your river there, what d'ye call it? Aye, Styx — Why 'tis as straight as Fleet Ditch. You should have given it a serpentine sweep, and sloped the banks of it. The place indeed has fine *capabilities*; but you should clear the wood to the left and clump the trees on the right. In short the whole wants variety, extent, contrast, inequality… Upon my word, here's a fine hah-hah! and a most curious collection of evergreens and flowering shrubs.

An artistic and literary circle, quite different from that of his inter-related aristocratic clients, now considered Brown worth noticing in their conversation and writing. And if he had acquired his nickname at Stowe, as I have suggested, it was becoming generally known.

Another commission (Madingley in Cambridgeshire for Sir John Hynde Cotton) came to Brown this year, and in 1757 he began work at two more great houses, both of these in the west. Probably the first — the exact date is uncertain — was Charlecote, the fine Tudor mansion which stands in an expanse of flat land on the banks of the Avon three miles east of Stratford.

Charlecote's owner, George Lucy, would have known of Brown from Admiral Anson of Moor Park — they were friends and Lucy had 'lit up his windows' to celebrate Anson's victory at Finisterre in 1747;[2] also from a neighbour, Lady Coventry of Snitterfield, who would have told him about Brown's dramatic transformation of the grounds of Croome Court, owned by her husband's cousin. Lucy

26. Longleat, Wiltshire.

was an amiable bachelor, much concerned with his own health, who was often abroad and even when in England spent long periods in Bath or London. But he wrote regular gossipy letters to Mrs Hayes, his housekeeper at Charlecote, which contain interesting mentions of Brown.[3]

Meanwhile Mrs Hayes kept a housebook in which she entered details of fowls supplied by tenants, fish caught in the river and work on the gardens.[4] From Lucy's letters, Mrs Hayes's book and Brown's contract with Lucy, the progress of his landscaping at Charlecote can be accurately followed.[5]

In the previous century Captain Thomas Lucy had given Charlecote a typical garden of the period, with a parterre between the house and the Wellesbourne, a nearby tributary of the Avon, and on the other side of the house a much larger Dutch water-garden with an orangery, all of which are shown in a painting of 1695.[6] It also shows long, double avenues of trees reaching north and south, the southern avenue starting across the Avon from the house. The trees appear to be conifers, but by the end of the century they must have been replaced by elms because, when these avenues died of Dutch elm disease in the mid 1970s, a typical tree was found to be two hundred and seventy-five years old.

The first improvements were carried out in the early 1750s, when Lucy was

27. The ha-ha at Charlecote, Warwickshire.

abroad. In 1752 and 1754 'firrs and oaks were planted in the park'.[7] Three years later in 1757 a local builder, Hiron, bridged the Wellesbourne close to its junction with the Avon. This bridge had a practical purpose for it gave Charlecote a better road to Stratford. It was only later that year when Lucy was about to return to England that he must have realised how unfashionable his garden had become. Though he did not reach Charlecote till July 1758 he had already used Brown. In September 1757 Mrs Hayes wrote that 'Mr Brown began to make alterations upon the Welsborn'.[8] The alterations consisted of a weir, referred to as a cascade, across the Wellesbourne below Hiron's bridge. This raised the level of the Wellesbourne some 10 feet and effectively cut off the deer in the south park from the house. It took about two years to complete. In March 1760 Lucy wrote from Bath, 'Pray how doth the Cascade look now it is finished?'.[9]

The same year Brown signed his contract with Lucy[10] and 'began to make the ground within the stable gates'.[11] In the contract he also undertook to widen the Avon, level its banks, create a ha-ha and plant trees at various places in the park. But by now Brown was in such demand that Charlecote got only a fraction of his attention. In March 1761 Lucy wrote from Bath: 'Mr Brown, who everyone wants, hath not yet made his appearance here, he is much wanted by a Mr Langton,[12] who you have heard us speak of, and who will have in a short time a most magnificent place, a new house by Mr Ledbeter, ground about it, laid out by Browne'.[13]

A fortnight later Lucy reported:

Mr Brown was here on Sunday last, and stayed till Tuesday, when he called upon me, not upon business, as he said, but to enquire after my health, and told me he should not be at Charlecote till May, which I suppose will be June at soonest. I did not well know how to construe this visit, I told him the time was elapsed for the second payment which he said was no matter, as he did not want money, but upon offering him a £100 note he pulled out his pocket book and carried it off with him. He tells me Langton's place will be good for nothing, owing to the obstinacy of its master.[14]

The meeting — which lasted only five minutes, Lucy added, before he had to hurry away — shows how Brown could now move among the rich and fashionable of Bath on easy and familiar terms.

At Charlecote, apart from building the weir, Brown turned the parterre to the east of the house beside the Wellesbourne into lawn, and turned Captain Thomas Lucy's Dutch water garden into a wilderness, planting it with pines. The painting of 1695 shows that the water garden was already on raised ground, but Brown simplified its surrounding ditch and brick wall, and extended this into a ha-ha running east, thus excluding the deer to the north of the house just as the Wellesbourne excluded them to the south. Today almost everything that Brown did at Charlecote can still be seen. His magnificent cedars stand beside the house and large herds of fallow deer roam the park beyond his ha-has.

If Charlecote is a fine house, set in a fine park, Longleat is on another scale. Familiar as Brown was by now with the estates of the wealthy, he must have been impressed. If he approached it from Warminster, as he may well have done, the house would have appeared suddenly lying far below him, at the centre of a vast saucer of hills, like the castle of some private kingdom.

By then this great house, built for Sir John Thynne in Elizabeth's reign, was one hundred and eighty years old. For at least one hundred and ten of these years the gardens had remained modestly formal. A painting by Jan Siberechts (1676)[15] shows, to the east of the house, merely a simple lawn enclosed by brick walls. But this was the side on which, during the next three decades, the gardens became grandly formal. Here the First Lord Weymouth employed London and Wise to lay out a Dutch garden crossed by a canal with many fountains and parterres. These extended beyond the canal, reaching up Park Hill.

The Second Viscount Weymouth, however, abandoned Longleat (he is said to have killed his wife's lover in a duel in an upper passage) to live in a house in the nearby village of Horningsham.[16] So when the Third Lord Weymouth succeeded him in 1756 at the age of eighteen he found the gardens neglected.

This young man's gaming and drinking were already well known. George II remarked to Lady Waldegrave that 'he could not be a good kind of man, as he never kept company with any women, and lived for nothing but play and strong beer'.[17] Horace Walpole called him 'an unconsiderable, debauched young man,... so minded to gaming that the moment before his exaltation he was setting out to France to avoid his creditors'.[18] His exaltation was his appointment in 1765 to be Viceroy of Ireland, but although he drew a £3000 payment he never went there. 'Sitting up nightly, gaming and drinking till six in the morning, and rising thus heated after noon, it was extraordinary that he was master of himself, or of what little he knew,' Walpole wrote. 'His great fortune he had damaged by such profuse play, that his house was often full of bailiffs.'[19] It is all the more remarkable that Brown appears to have had an untroubled business relationship with him lasting six years, and to have been paid regularly and in full, a total of £6,131 15s.[20]

Brown made four contracts with Weymouth, the first in 1757, the last in 1762. They give a clear picture of the way in which he co-operated with his clients and provided them with what they wanted. They refer regularly to stakes set in the ground to mark the extent of some lake or feature. During 1757 Brown and Weymouth must have spent many hours riding around the grounds, agreeing about the placing of these stakes; for each contract they must have gone through the same process.

Central to the plan was the sweeping away of London's and Wise's parterres, and the transformation of their canal into the string of lakes which survive today. These were principally to be ornamental, but had practical purposes. One of the upper ones was to have 'a head of sixteen feet perpendicular in order to make it flow up to where the park pale now stands... NB The reason for so great a head is to make the water a reservoir for supplying the intended offices and for occasionally

28. Longleat, set 'like the castle of some private kingdom'.

to clean the drains of the house and to float the meadows.'[21]

Sunk fences are regularly mentioned, and in one paragraph the phrase is defined. Brown was to 'build in it a wall of brick, stone and lime sufficient to keep out the deer and support the earth. NB six feet high is a sufficient fence.'[22]

Brown was also to adorn the verges of a path to the kitchen garden with 'shrubs, trees of curious sorts and turf', but for Longleat, unlike Petworth, no plant list survives. In the kitchen garden he was to make three stews for fish.

Throughout, Weymouth's own responsibilities are carefully defined. He was invariably to supply horses and carts with harness. A particularly rough piece of ground he was to plough with his oxen. He was also to supply trees. Just how many we don't know, but for what were probably six typical years in the 1770s they varied between 35,864 (winter of 1776) and 91,258 (winter of 1773). In a typical year (1772) mostly oak were used, but conifers were also planted, including 'Scots firrs', 'silver firrs', 'spruce firrs', and Weymouth pines, these last originally imported from North America by the First Lord Weymouth. Oddly, no elms are mentioned, but elms were certainly used at Longleat because in one contract Brown agreed 'to transport all the young elms in the Garden... to such places as shall be thought of most advantage'.[23]

Elsewhere he agreed to sow a particular area with Dutch clover and grass seed, or to lay turf, and 'shou'd any part of it fail' to sow it over again 'till it does answer'. He also undertook to make and unmake various roads and to drain ground, at one point 'making use of the materials of the old road for the drains and for making the new road'.[24] The drains would have consisted of narrow channels filled with the stones of the old road then capped.

Brown's landscape at Longleat survives virtually intact. The pleasure walk, with its views of the house, has recently been remade and is lined with many curious trees, though not all of them would have been available to Brown and he would have used shrubs as ground cover. The famous safari park has been kept decently out of sight to the north of the house, and if sea-lions sport in the wake of the pleasure boats on Brown's largest lake, exotic animals and menageries were much in the tradition of Brown's day.

Horace Walpole, who came to Longleat in 1762 before the work was finished, made one of his grumpier comments: 'In the park is the original Weymouth Pine, from the cones of which all the Weymouth pines have come: it is now very shabby. The water is not well contrived, the ponds do not unite well and the cascades have not water enough. There is a new garden making, and a gate built, designed by Brown, too small, and in a false taste'.[25] Though Weymouth was not one of those who signed the petition of 1758, there is no reason to think that he found fault with Brown's work.

In 1761 Weymouth and another of Brown's clients, Dacre of Belhus, were strangely brought together. They corresponded when both were refused tickets to George III's coronation because they had both said that they were physically unable to walk in the procession. Dacre was only forty-five and Weymouth a mere twenty-three.[26]

It was almost certainly in the year that Brown first went to Longleat (1757) that he went to Wotton in Buckinghamshire to landscape on an equally large scale. His employer here was George Grenville, younger brother of Richard. Their mother, Cobham's sister, had inherited Stowe when Cobham died (this unusual succession had been arranged when Cobham became a viscount, as if he already knew that he would have no children — he took doses of red mercury and may have suffered from venereal disease).[27] Now that their mother had also died, her elder son,

29. Sunlight on the great stretch of water at Wotton, Buckinghamshire.

Richard, had moved to Stowe, thus leaving George at Wotton. It was Richard's move to Stowe with his own gardener in 1751 which had left no position there for Brown. But the two brothers, Richard and George, remained closely in touch. They would ride to meet each other at an inn at Three Bridges, a half-way point,[28] and they shared an interest in landscaping.

George Grenville was a dull and unimaginative character. George III complained that when Grenville had 'wearied me for two hours... he looks at his watch, to see if he may not tire me for an hour more'.[29] According to Horace Walpole, Grenville's political ambition was equal to Pitt's, but 'his plodding, methodic genius made him take the spirit of detail for ability'.[30]

The house he had taken over at Wotton had been built for his grandfather in 1704, at the summit of a low hill which gave its grounds exactly the potential which Brown so often exploited. To the east they stretched away to the distant hills around Waddesdon. To the west they sloped down to a shallow valley, where a Tudor map shows a stream and two pieces of water, one triangular, one rectangular, before rising to Brill and Muswell Hills. In about 1709 George London had laid out parterres near the house, planted long avenues to the north, south, east and — more importantly for what was to survive — to the west, where a double line of elms reached down into the valley.

In the 1740s when Brown was still at Stowe, he had received occasional payments from Richard Grenville which used to be taken as evidence that it was then that he landscaped Wotton.[31] But there is no other evidence that George London's layout was changed at this time and it now seems more likely that these were tips for showing Grenville's visitors round Stowe or at most for small-scale garden improvements. Newly found papers show that in 1757 and 1758 Brown received from George Grenville three much larger payments of £100 each.[32] They strongly suggest that these were the years in which he did his major work at Wotton.

Where the great western avenue dipped into the valley he created two miles of intricately connected lakes, canals and artificial rivers. If the result is complex, so must its designing have been, since water flows out of both ends of this system of waterways. Some arrives from the hills, but a large amount comes probably from natural springs in the two lakes.

Thomas Whately, in his *Observations on Modern Gardening*, published some thirteen years later in 1771, gives a full description of the experience of walking beside Wotton's two miles of waterway. First comes a river 'flowing through a lovely mead, open in some places to views of beautiful hills in the country, and adorned in others with clumps of trees, so large their branches stretch quite across, and form a high arch over the water'. Next comes a once-formal basin of fourteen acres, which subdivides and leads to terminations 'so artfully concealed, that the deception is never suspected'. Third comes a longer stretch of river, 'everywhere broad, and its course... such as to admit of infinite variety, without any confusion'. Here is 'a very beautiful grove of oaks, scattered over a green swerd of extraordinary verdure'. This three-quarter-mile walk retains 'at all times a mildness of character, which is still more forcibly felt when the shadows grow faint as they lengthen; when a little rustling of birds in the spray, the leaping of fish, and the fragrancy of the woodbine, denote the approach of evening'. Finally comes the major lake, with a tall island and Ionic portico, an elegant bridge, an octagonal building and a Chinese room. Here 'a profusion of water pours in from all sides round upon the view.'[33]

About twenty-five years ago Wotton was due to be demolished. Permission had been granted for a housing estate on the site and Brown's landscape had already been split into eight holdings when the present owner, with a fortnight to spare, intervened. As a result the house was saved, the landscape is now re-united and Thomas Whately's walk can be followed almost precisely as he describes it. True, the bridge and island temple have gone, the octagonal building is derelict and the Chinese Pavilion has been sold to America during the last thirty-five years,[34] but two temples, not there in Whately's time, at the end of the once-formal basin have been rebuilt and a Turkish Pavilion soon will be.

The gardens at Wotton are interesting because, in spite of their scale and naturalness, they have some of the character of a pleasure garden. On a map of 1789 they are described as 'The Marquess of Buckingham's seat and Pleasure Ground'. Although Whately does not justify his admiration for Wotton on the grounds that its features stimulate noble sentiments or improve the mind, he moves

VIII. The house overlooking the lake at Wotton, Buckinghamshire.

IX. (Overleaf) Longleat, Wiltshire.

X. The huge, layered, oriental plane tree (*Platanus orientalis insularis [cretica]*) at Corsham Court, Wiltshire.

XI. Chatsworth, Derbyshire.

along the banks of river and lake examining the feelings which feature after feature arouse, only mentioning their unity as an afterthought and the house not at all.

He had reason since, except from the foot of the western avenue, it is scarcely visible. From the main lake only its chimney pots can be glimpsed above the tree tops. This is a garden in which the nobleman could wander for his pleasure, as he still might in its present form of a nature reserve.

From the house, however, Wotton seems pre-eminently a Brown garden. Its great lawn sweeps down to the water's edge across undulating lawns which are full of curve and movement. A stone ha-ha excludes the cattle which have been given raised pieces of ground to mount, to increase the impression that they are *in* the garden. Across the water stand encircling woods and beyond them encircling hills.

There is another reason for believing that Brown landscaped Wotton when it was George Grenville's. Grenville signed the petition of 1758 in support of Brown. He was the only commoner to do so.

The other thirteen names show how widely Brown was now known and admired. Seven are unsurprising. Anson of Moor Park, Temple (Richard Grenville) of Stowe, Egremont of Petworth, Exeter of Burghley, Coventry of Croome, Brooke of Warwick and Northumberland of Syon and Alnwick had all employed Brown to landscape or build for them. Four more, however — Ashburnham of Ashburnham, Ancaster of Grimsthorpe, Hertford of Ragley and Midleton of Peper Harow, did not employ him till later, and there is no evidence that he ever worked for the final two, Holdernesse of Syon Hill and Stamford of Enville.

The petition was submitted to the Prime Minister, the Duke of Newcastle. The fourteen, 'being well-wishers of Mr Browne, whose abilities and merit we are fully acquainted with, do most earnestly request the Duke of Newcastle to promote his speedy appointment to the care of Kensington Garden agreeable to his Grace's very obliging promises in that respect, the delay having already occasion'd great loss to Mr Browne in his business and great inconvenience to many persons for whom he is employed.'[35]

The form of words is curious. Precisely how Brown's business had suffered is not obvious. What he needed was not more or more profitable business, but the honour which a royal appointment would bring him. He was now forty-two and his patrons felt he deserved it. But the Duke of Newcastle did nothing.

The royal gardener at Kensington was one of three, the others managing Windsor and Hampton Court. Eventually in 1760 Dr John Hill was given the job Brown had hoped for. Horace Walpole wrote: 'I am sorry to say this journeyman is one of the first men preferred in the new reign: he is made gardener of Kensington, a place worth £2000 a year'.[36]

The following year, 1759, Brown took on work for another client whose private life was to give him problems. This was the Duke of Bridgewater, owner of Ashridge in Hertfordshire, the house in which Edward VI and Elizabeth had spent some of their childhoods. The park's mile-long Prince's Riding was probably named after

Edward when he was Prince of Wales. Elizabeth retired to Ashridge when Mary became queen, and here she was arrested on suspicion of being involved with Wyatt's rebellion.[37]

Bridgewater had been twelve when he inherited from his brother his title and property. His father had died when he was young and his mother (who then married Sir Richard Lyttelton — nephew of Richard and George Grenville) had neglected him. He was sent on a foreign tour with the orientalist, Robert Wood, who persuaded him to buy various marbles in Rome. They interested him so little that they were found still in their packing cases when he died.[38]

At the age of 23 (1759) he had become engaged to Elizabeth, the younger of the two beautiful Gunning sisters, who was now a widow since her first husband, the impetuous and infatuated Duke of Hamilton, had died. Meanwhile, however, the affair which her elder sister, Lady Coventry, was having with Lord Bolingbroke had become notorious,[39] and, according to family tradition, Bridgewater forbade his fiancée, Elizabeth, to see her sister after their marriage.[40] When Elizabeth refused to obey, the Duke is said to have abandoned Ashridge and gone to live at Worsley in Lancashire. Here he built the Bridgewater Canal, which, with other canals, was to earn him the name of 'Father of Inland Waterways'. His monument today stands at the western end of Prince's Riding.

With the Duke of Bridgewater usually absent, Brown perhaps gave less attention than he might otherwise have done to the landscaping of Ashridge. If he had attempted a typical Brown landscape he would anyway have had one serious problem. There was no river near, and such a chronic shortage of water that, before the Reformation, dogs 'working in the same manner as a turnspit' had raised water from a deep well, and after the Restoration a horse walking in a wheel.[41] He did, however, work on the Golden Valley, a dramatic natural feature out of sight of the house, thinning and adjusting the trees on its sides. And his account book records the building of a garden wall.

His accounts also suggest that arrangements for rebuilding the house were firmer, and the work continued for many years. In 1759 and 1760 Brown had made several journeys and submitted four plans for the house and two uprights. For these and the building work he was paid a total of almost £3000, the last payment in 1768. This was one of the projects in which Henry Holland, his builder friend of Fulham, was involved. Today, whatever Brown did to the gardens on the spur of land behind the house, has been obliterated by Humphry Repton's work there, and the house itself, now a management training college, was entirely rebuilt in 1800.

Even though little remains of Brown's work at Ashridge, his connection with Bridgewater is of much interest. Brown had already been making artificial lakes and rivers for almost twenty years. Bridgewater was to spend the rest of his life making canals. During the nine years that they had dealings with each other, they can hardly have failed to discuss the problems of this new technology. The Duke could well have learned from Brown. And when, in 1764, Brown began to work at Blenheim, he may have been inspired by the Duke to build the newly identified

30. James Paine's bridge, central feature of Brown's landscape at Chatsworth, Derbyshire.

canal which is one of the less known features of his work there.

The following year (1760) Brown began work on two important but entirely different commissions: the grounds at Chatsworth in Derbyshire, and the house and grounds at Corsham in Wiltshire. As a pair — Chatsworth with its vast sweeps

of parkland and encircling plantations, Corsham with its ornate picture gallery ceiling — they well suggest the range of his abilities.

Chatsworth, home of the Dukes of Devonshire, had already by the end of the seventeenth century (c.1694) been given its most remarkable garden feature: Grillet's Great Cascade. This descends the hillside which rises abruptly to the east of the house, in a succession of wide stone steps. Brown left the cascade but smoothed into lawn the terraces beside it and began the planting of the bare hillside above, which Joseph Paxton continued in the next century and which now covers it to its crest.

Closer to the house, to the south, London and Wise had created extensive parterres and 'many foolish waterworks'.[42] Brown completed the sweeping away of all but one of these, the Seahorse Fountain. To the west he levelled more parterres, bringing the house into direct contact with the low-lying parkland beside the River Derwent. The river he realigned and raised, and across the park laid a new drive for which James Paine built a three-arched stone bridge. Though some formal gardens have been re-established near the house, Brown's landscaping of the riverside parkland and planting beyond have survived and are today a mature version of one of his finest works. Paine's bridge is its central feature; only a very slight alteration of its angle to the house would have spoiled the effect.

For ecologists the Great Slope beside the cascade which Brown smoothed into lawns has a special interest. In Oliver Gilbert's words, it is 'a most remarkable area with a dense, springy, moss-rich turf containing an extremely wide diversity of plants, many of which are rarely seen on lawns'. Its history has recently been studied and Brown's method discovered. He used no turf, but hayseed, bought at Sheffield. Later he rolled and harrowed the ground, and that was all.[43] During the following two hundred and twenty years it was first cut by scythe, then from 1833 by horse-drawn mower and finally by motor mower, but no fertilizer, lime or herbicide ever applied. In 1983 the Sports Turf Research Council prepared a plan to cure the lawn's weediness, which was only at the last moment cancelled when the present Duke learned about the rarity of his Brown lawn.[44]

At Corsham, which lay close to the Wiltshire village of that name, just south of the Bath road, Brown was employed by Paul Methuen to landscape but principally to build. Methuen's house was a modest Elizabethan one, set at the edge of an equally modest square of land. He believed, correctly as it turned out, that he was going to inherit a fine collection of paintings from his cousin and god-father, *Sir Paul Methuen*, who had been British Ambassador in Lisbon and had helped to arrange Britain's port wine treaty with Portugal, but only on condition that they would be properly housed. He therefore needed a large picture gallery; although Brown added a number of other rooms at Corsham, and landscaped the grounds, everything he did there was centred on this gallery. It formed the main ground-floor room of the new east wing which he added; its windows gave the best view of the grounds. Methuen and his visitors were perhaps meant to look from paintings by Claude Lorrain and Salvator Rosa to a view of the sort of real-life landscape

31. Brown designed the Gothic Bath House at Corsham Court, Wiltshire, but it was later altered by John Nash.

which such paintings had inspired.

As so often, Brown planned a lake, this one to be set at the far side of the grounds from the house, and to take the form of a large oval pond rather than a mock river. As at several other places, he never made the lake, but fortunately at Corsham, Humphry Repton later made one in the same place of a similar shape. To give a clear view of the proposed lake from the house Brown removed hedges, roadways and inconvenient cottages, and re-divided the park with a sunk fence (literally a fence sunk in a ditch).

To the north of the house, however, he left an old elm avenue, where it appeared to be a driveway from the Bath road to the front of the house. There are two reasons for finding this surprising: it was clearly not meant to be an actual drive, for he built a ha-ha cutting it off from the house; it also blocked views across the park from the North Walk, which runs parallel but nearer to the village. Just how pleasant these views are, across an expanse of parkland now set with the immense oaks which he planted, as far as his encircling belt of trees, has been obvious since the mid 1970s when the elms all died of Dutch elm disease.

Brown ordered trees for Corsham from Kennedy and Lee, the nursery near his home in Hammersmith.[45] Of all that Brown did in the grounds of Corsham (where he also built a Gothic Bath House and a cattle tunnel) it is a tree which has become most remarkable. The great oriental plane, standing just within the ha-ha, is said to cover half an acre and to have a circumference of 240 yards. All around it, branches have dipped to the ground where they have layered to produce subsidiary trees, each large in itself.

Brown's picture gallery in the east wing is equally remarkable, partly for its size (72 feet by 24 feet) but more for its ceiling. This astonishing piece of plaster work, restored in 1984 after the supporting joists had started to collapse from death-watch beetle damage, with its *putti*, fruit and baskets of flowers in high relief, was originally designed for the hall at Burton Constable in Yorkshire, but rejected.[46] Brown had reason to be proud of it, and was no doubt glad of the chance to offer it to Methuen who wisely accepted it.

To do the work Brown used a Bristol craftsman, Thomas Stocking, who also plastered other new rooms in the house. A letter from Stocking to Brown suggests how the problems of his craft were increased when dealing with Brown, who was now overworked and often ill.

I make bold to trouble you with this to beg the favour of sending me down the drawings for the drawing room vestiable, the cornice of the two later are finish'd.

I have been obliged to keep my ornament stands on mouldings for sum time past which is hurtful to mee, and at this time wee have nothing to do, and the cieling of the cove bedchamber will be too dry to recive the ornaments, if wee don't recive them soon. I shall be extreemly glad if you'll send them to Corsham as soon as you are at leasure...[47]

32. Brown's glorious plaster-work ceiling in the picture gallery of Corsham Court.

When, four months later in March 1764, Brown wrote to Methuen asking him to give Stocking the plans, he concluded: 'I cough night and day. I mean to take a little journey by way of changing the air'.[48]

Brown had also been ill at the start of his work at Corsham. In September 1761 he wrote to Methuen: 'My health which has been extreamly bad is now on the mending hand and I hope soon to be quite stout'. He continued: 'but the Queen's not coming has made an exceeding great tumble in my business'.[49] Just why the delay in the arrival of Princess Charlotte from Mecklenburg (where among others Elizabeth Gunning, the Duke of Bridgewater's ex-fiancée, now Lady of the Bed-chamber, had gone to fetch her) should have affected Brown's business is not clear. The remark was probably the sort which any self-employed professional makes from time to time about his financial prospects. By 1760 Brown had worked on, or was actively preparing to work on, at least thirty-six commissions, and many of these were to continue for years.[50]

The same financial caution must explain why he had taken no assistant but was still himself doing all the planning, accounting, letter-writing, travelling and surveying from his house in Hammersmith Mall.

As for his reputation, though he was still to create most of the landscapes for which he is best remembered today, this was now at its height. To Lord Shelburne of Bowood, writing in 1757, he was already 'the famous Mr Brown'.

6. Royal Gardener

 'WHAT WOU'D YOU GIVE to know the consequences of the visit of the famous Mr Brown and the fruit of the 30 guineas which I gave him?' Lord Shelburne had written. 'He passed two days with me… and twenty times assured me that he does not know of a finer place in England than Bowood Park [Wiltshire], and that he is sure no prince in Europe has so fine a fruit garden.' There had so far been no consequences, Shelburne continued, but he was 'persuaded that the man means to present me at some future time with a well-digested plan for this place, and perhaps to come to me to explain it'.[1]

A scheme of work must in fact have been agreed by 1761, because in April Shelburne paid Brown £500,[2] but typically the final plan was not ready for another two years. By this time the First Earl had died. Brown provided the planting around the mausoleum which Adam built for him, high up at the western end of the estate.

As a result it was with the much more politically active Second Earl that Brown signed his contract and became chiefly involved. The young Shelburne was twenty-four when he inherited Bowood, and had already fought as a colonel in Germany during the Seven Years War. He had also become a Member of Parliament for Chipping Wycombe, and while Brown worked at Bowood he was at different times President of the Board of Trade (1763) and Secretary of State (1766 to 1768). Later he became Home Secretary (1782) and finally in 1782-3 he was Prime Minister for ten months. He is often described as a Tory radical, and his principles in part explain his relatively brief periods in office. He did not belong, as did many of Brown's clients, to the great interconnected and interrelated Whig families of the time. By them he was considered devious and untrustworthy. Instead he formed a group of dissenters, radicals and innovators known as the 'Bowood Circle' with whom he was more in sympathy. But he recognised the effect that these friends had on his career. 'It has been my fate through life,' he wrote, 'always to fall in with clever but unpopular connections.'[3]

If Shelburne had been more successful as a politician, and therefore more in

33. Brown's plan for Bowood, Wiltshire, refers to a rockwork cascade at the head of the new lake. It was not built until 1785, and then to a design by Charles Hamilton.

London, we might have the detailed letters of a head gardener or steward describing the making of the gardens at Bowood which are so valuable for two of Brown's later gardens, Harewood and Tottenham. But the diary of Shelburne's first wife, Sofia Cartaret, is an excellent substitute. It conveys some of the excitement which many of Brown's clients must have felt as they saw his schemes transform their grounds.

On 30 May 1765 Lady Shelburne wrote: 'There remains to finish the offices and to form a considerable piece of water on the head of which they are now at work... Mr Browne's plantations are very young but promising'.[4] Brown was at Bowood again on 5 August that year when he 'spent the evening in giving directions to his man' (not 'men' as sometimes transcribed).

On 24 March the next year Lady Shelburne and friends 'not withstanding the cold walk'd down to the head of the Great Water which was finish'd and beginning to be fill'd'. And on 17 June, 'As soon as breakfast was over we took a walk and were vastly pleas'd with the effect of the water which flows into a magnificent river and only wants more to rise to its proper height which it comes nearer to every day.'

A fortnight later there had been more than enough. 'I walk'd... down to the head which had nearly been overflow'd by the extraordinary rain, that they have been forced to make passage for some of the water into farmer Carlings field.'

Just what a problem the very large dam — some 30 feet high at the centre and 150 yards long — had been to build she does not mention. The Shelburne land ran out at the point where it was needed, and as a result it had to be crushed up against the boundary. Today a fine cascade here dramatizes the outflow from Brown's lake, but it was not made till a couple of years after his death.

Nor was the little, much photographed, temple yet set on its hilltop at this end of the lake (see page 94). It was moved to this position in the nineteenth century. Now, backed by the tall beeches which Brown planted here, as well as on top of the dam, it makes perhaps the finest of all the set pieces in Brown's many landscapes.

The stream which this, the main dam, holds up is the Whetham Brook. Higher up, Brown made a smaller lake from the Washway Stream, by damming this where it joins the Whetham. Neither lake was made precisely as shown on his plan.[5] At the upper end of each a filter pond was added. They have proved so effective that in the following two hundred and twenty years neither lake has had to be dredged.

Once the main lake was finished Brown went to work on 'levelling the lawn to the edge of the water'. By 10 July 1768, however, things had gone backwards. Lady Shelburne found 'the place in perfect good order except the necessity that there has been of letting out the water which has not yet had time to fill'. 'The Menagerie,' she added, had 'increas'd extremely.' Here the Shelburnes kept, among other animals, tigers. Just what the trouble had been with the lake, we don't know, but it had still not been cured by the end of the following May, when Lord Shelburne 'left directions that the water and the ground before the house to be finish'd by the time

34. Bowood House from the lake.

we must return there at Michaelmas'.

Meanwhile Brown completed the planting of his peripheral belt of trees and of the trees around the Mausoleum. His orders for trees included larches, ash, quickset (hawthorn) and elm, but it is his magnificent beeches which, in the main, survive here today. From the nineteenth century onwards rhododendrons have been planted among them, and in the 1930s some were felled to create a clear space around the Mausoleum and others to give a view of the lake below, but the setting remains a fine one and, except at rhododendron blossoming time, must represent Brown's hopes for it at full maturity.

In 1955 the Eighth Marquess of Lansdowne knocked down the Big House, leaving only a lower wing and stables. As a result a first time visitor feels something is missing — as indeed it is. Bowood confirms that the great houses around which Brown landscaped were not just viewpoints but important landscape features. Despite its much reduced mansion, Bowood, with its lawns sweeping down to its lake which stretches out of sight in both directions like some vast river, remains one of Brown's most magnificent achievements.

35. The Tudor house of Temple Newsam, Leeds, stands high above the valley.

1761, the year in which Brown began his great work at Bowood, was also the year in which he took one more step in his steady advance from garden boy to gentleman. In September he sent his eldest son, called Lance in the family to distinguish him from his father, to Eton. Here the boy soon became known as 'Capey'.[6] Brown's nickname was now familiar even to schoolboys. It was also probably in 1761, despite the serious illness which he described in his letter to Methuen at Corsham, that he extended his practice in the North by undertaking to landscape Temple Newsam for Charles Ingram, later Viscount Irwin.

Irwin (as it will be convenient to call him) had first asked Brown to visit him three years earlier,[7] when Brown had replied that he could not call before the next summer; but in fact he probably did not come till 1761. Certainly it was not till January 1763 that Irwin wrote to Brown to say that he was pleased to hear that plans were ready, and would Brown send them as soon as possible by the 'Leeds Machine' which left from the Swan and Two Necks in Lord Lane and was 'the most expeditious way'.[8]

Irwin's great Tudor house, sometimes described as the Hampton Court of the North, stands in a fine position, high above the valley of a small tributary of the River Aire, though just how fine it is now hard to judge, since the whole south-eastern skyline is dominated by a mountain of bare slag. Open-cast mining at one time came even closer to the house so that it is also hard to be sure whether or not the re-sown hillside which swells up in this direction has its original shape. Whether it does or not, the five new clumps which have been planted here, in a worthy attempt to recreate Brown's landscape, are surprisingly successful. They have the elegance of an eighteenth century print (see page 96), and are certainly more like those which Brown saw during his lifetime than those which survive and sometimes seem overmature.

Apart from the slag mountain, the saddest thing (among a great many at Temple Newsam today) is that the lake which Brown planned in the valley bottom was never made. The small surviving ponds, the work of an earlier Yorkshire gardener, William Etty, are largely hidden in neglected woodland.

Visitors had been looking forward to the lake since it was first proposed:

> But when the Lake shall these sweet Groves adorn
> And light expanding like the eye of Morn
> Reflects whate'er above its surface rise
> The Hills, the Rocks, the Woods, and varying Skies
> Then will the wild and beautiful combine
> And taste and Beauty grace your whole Design.[9]

This poem, of which there is much more, was published anonymously in 1767 and dedicated to Irwin. It is presumably the one referred to by Sidney Swinney, in a letter to Irwin of 5 June 1765: 'In consequence of your Lordship's advice, I am going to forbid the publication of my poetical performance, 'til my return to Town, which will be immediately upon a summons, from you, or Mr Browne. The favourable manner in which you was pleased to receive the *declaration*, I just made to you, gives me hopes it is not less in your inclination, than your power to befriend me, in my distress...'[10]

Perhaps Irwin (and Brown) had wanted the poem's publication postponed because they, too, were hoping that the lake would materialize and the lines describing it would need rewriting.

As well as the lake, Brown planned sham bridges, a rotunda, a menagerie, a cottage and a dairy. These seem to have been built but none survive. All that does is an ornamental iron gate, and a small temple, across the valley from the house, now much defaced by graffiti of visitors from Leeds, for whom Temple Newsam is now an official playground.

Brown was still being paid by Irwin in 1770, but a letter of the previous October suggests that his work at Temple Newsam had been taken as far as Irwin wanted. If anything was needed at 'the Temple', Brown wrote, his man was at Lord Scarbrough's (at Sandbeck forty miles to the south) and would come over.[11]

Bowood was only one of a fairly large number of Brown's schemes in which he had technical trouble with his water works. It is all the more surprising that this clients rarely complained about his work, his charges or any other part of their business connections with him. But in 1762 he undertook work at the famous Essex house of Audley End, near Saffron Walden, for Sir John Griffin Griffin, who was to prove an exception. Perhaps Griffin was an exceptionally difficult client. Like Cobham of

Stowe, he had been a soldier, and had only retired after being severely wounded at the battle of Campen in Germany.[12] Like Cobham, he had no children and took a keen personal interest in improving his property: 'I imagine you,' William Pitt wrote to Griffin, soon after Griffin's retirement to Audley End, 'deeply engaged in the amusing cares of building, planting and decorating etc.'[13]

Sir John Griffin Griffin had inherited his property from his aunt, the Countess of Portsmouth, at the age of forty-three, on condition that he changed his name from Whitwell to her family one of Griffin. Though the house, which had been built by the First Earl of Suffolk on the site of a monastery, and had once been 'by far the grandest Jacobean building of Essex and one of the biggest Jacobean mansions of England',[14] was now much reduced, nothing could alter its delightful setting, surrounded by low hills in the valley of the upper Cam. The Cam was the main feature of its grounds, crossing from south to north a couple of hundred yards in front of the house. Because the house stood very little above it, the grounds were an opportunity for Brown to show that he could create a park of a very different character from those in which the house looked out over a natural valley.

The Cam was the first feature which Brown agreed to improve. In his contract of 1763 he undertook to widen this in front of the house, as well as to the south of a new bridge. Six other items amounted in sum to setting the elongated lake which this part of the Cam now became across a great ellipse of lawn, which was to be surrounded by clumps and belts of trees. New carriageways were to approach the house down each side of the ellipse, crossing the lake at either end. Beyond, planting was to continue up the hillside, as it was to the rear of the house, where there was to be a ha-ha.[15] All was to emphasize the sense of the house being set in a great secluded dell — and all was to be completed in thirteen months.

Not surprisingly, it wasn't. But Brown and Griffin came to a gentleman's agreement by which Griffin released Brown from his contractual obligations, and Brown continued with the work, charging Griffin the cost as this progressed. Beyond the original two instalments of £200 each, Griffin paid Brown another £400, then another £200 (according to Griffin, but Brown did not deny it). When Brown submitted his final account, however, this came to a further £304 9s 2d, and included the following item: 'Taken upon an average that Sir John Griffin never owed me less than four hundred pounds for 3 years at 5 per cent — £60.' Subsequently Brown calculated the interest 'on a different principal' and reduced it to £36 6s 0d, and Griffin paid this as part of the total settlement on 14 May that year.[16] But he remained aggrieved, and drew up a four-page memorandum setting out his case. After mentioning the contract's completion date and the dates the first two instalments of £200 were paid, he continued:

The work instead of being finished in May 1764 — was very backward at the latter end of 1764 — when I was neither satisfied with the delay, nor with the manner in which some of it's parts were finishing...

In May 1765 I paid Mr Brown £400 for work going on; and in May 1766 £200 more on the same account and he knows I was always ready and did advance at

36. Sir John Griffin Griffin by Biagio Rebecca.

any time he ask'd it what money he called for and never refus'd him payment...

In April or May 1766 I received his account when it appear'd there was a ballance in Mr B's favour of £94 9s 4d. From this time May 1766... to the final settling of our account in May 1767 — he never advanced one shilling – for I paid the labourers and his foreman as the work went on.

What right therefore Mr B has to charge interest for money advanc'd for my works, and at what rate — must be determin'd by less partial judges than myself...

NB I allow Mr B his own charges for his trouble... of £150 — and take no notice of the injury done to the work by giving a wrong bend to the river, and contrary to his own plan...

Brown replied on 7 October 1767, claiming that he had tried several times to deliver the supporting papers to Griffin but found him out; and justifying his claim for interest:

I have looked that paper over which you gave me and by no means approve of it... I am very sure I never employed less than three hundred pounds on your account... Amongst my accounts I find sold out of the three per-cents eight hundred pounds to carry on Sir — and Sir John Griffin Griffin's work, you judge whether I put that money into Mr Drummonds hands at thirty pounds at a time, I assure you I cannot humble my mind to act on so narrow a principal, I dare say if I could I should have been richer and perhaps wiser...

For some months he had no answer, but in February 1768 he and Griffin exchanged their final notes. By now they were addressing each other in the third person. On 1 February Griffin wrote:

Sir John Griffin receiv'd Mr Brown's letter and though it requires no answer, yet as a total silence might perhaps induce him to think Sir John was better satisfied than he was before the receipt of his Letter, in regard to the interest mony he refers to, he takes this opportunity of saying he has the same opinion of that matter that he ever had.

On 11 February Brown replied:

Mr Brown informes Sir John Griffen that he has received his note and as Sir John meant to say nothing that was agreeable to Mr Brown, after 7 months silence it would have been as well to let it sleep on; Mr Brown had neither thought of Sir John nor the money from that time to this and had forgot and forgave,... but at the same time assures Sir John that he continues in the same mind in regard to the interest, and thinks himself not honourably treated in that respect. Mr Brown will never labour more to convince Sir John, as he knows there is none so blind as him that will not see.

The whole incident is a strange one. Brown rarely if ever charged interest on his outlay, and it is hard to understand why he did so on this occasion, unless Griffin

XII. The view from the nineteenth century parterre beside Bowood House, Wiltshire, to the calm beauty of Brown's parkland beyond.

XIII. (Overleaf) Bowood. The little Doric Temple, beautifully positioned to be reflected in Brown's lake, was placed here in 1864.

XIV. New clumps of trees planted in Brown's style at Temple Newsam, Leeds.

XV. Audley End, Essex.

was being slower to meet Brown's expenses than he claimed.

Though this quarrel brought Brown's work at Audley End to a premature conclusion, and it was Adam who added a bridge, stable block and garden temples, and Joseph Hicks who improved the shape of the lake, all was done under the influence of Brown's original plan. In 1797 Mr de Lelyveld came to Audley End, and his account suggests the dramatic first impression it made on him. By then the carriage drive was thickly enclosed with trees. When a visitor emerged from these 'a splendid amphitheatre takes his breath away'. Much the same could be said about a first sight of Audley End today.

By coincidence, Brown also quarrelled in a briefer but more dramatic way with another East Anglian client, Ambrose Dickens of Branches. Dickens added a sum of £59 1s 8d to Brown's bill for work which *he* had authorized but Brown had not. Brown noted in his account book: 'Mr Brown could not get the money for extra work and tore the account before Mr Dickens face and said his say upon that business to him'.[17] It has been suggested[18] that Dickens and Griffin, as neighbours, grumbled together about Brown, but their seats were twenty-five miles apart, and the quarrel with Dickens was in 1765, while that with Griffin in 1767.

There is perhaps a better explanation. For ten or fifteen years now, Brown had been in demand by the leading families of the land. All over England he had been not just gardening but transforming great tracts of countryside to conform with his own vision. He was currently engaged on his best known and most spectacular work of all for the Duke of Marlborough at Blenheim. It is hardly surprising that such success should temporarily have gone to the head of a poor country boy from a hamlet in remotest Northumberland

It was to his native county that Brown now returned to work for the Duke of Northumberland on the landscaping of his castle at Alnwick. The Duke (Sir Hugh Smithson till 1766) was one of the richest men in the country. According to Horace Walpole he had 'much courtesy in his address, which being supported by the most expensive magnificence, made him exceedingly popular with the meaner sort'. The Duchess was an equally flamboyant character, 'a jovial heap of contradictions,' her person 'more vulgar than anything but her conversation, which was larded indiscriminately with stories of her ancestry and her footmen. Show, crowds, and junketing, were her endless pursuit'.[19] Together they lived 'by the etiquette of the old peerage, they have Swiss porters, the countess has her pipers — in short they will soon have no estate'. Though by 1752 the Duke was already 'building at Northumberland House, Sion, Stanstead, Alnwick Castle and Wentworth Castle'[20] Walpole proved wrong and the estate survived.

At Alnwick, close to the Scottish borders, the castle stood, and still stands, on a rocky hill at the edge of the town, looking out across the River Aln to open country. Here the Duchess, who was particularly keen on Gothic, employed James Paine and Robert Adam to embellish the interior with highly ornate Gothic stucco work. Huge Gothic windows were let into the mediaeval castle walls and a beautiful,

37. Hugh, 1st Duke of Northumberland, by Thomas
Gainsborough, c. 1783. (By
courtesy of His Grace the
Duke of Northumberland.)

new, fan-shaped staircase built. Such improvements were intended to make the castle into a family home. To the curtain walls turrets were added, set with numerous stone figures in imitation of earlier mediaeval ones.

In parallel with such bizarre alterations, Brown worked on the grounds. A Canaletto painting of about 1750 shows the rough slope with outcropping rocks which at that time descended below the castle to the river. A Watts engraving of 1783 shows that this was transformed into smooth, green, treeless lawn. Brown filled a small side-stream, the Bow Burn, to make a terrace walk, and widened the river. He no doubt also advised the Duke about the numerous trees he planted — twelve hundred every year for twenty years.[21]

Travellers of the time admired the results of Brown's work. In 1774, Walter Stanhope, a local landowner, wrote that if the Duke 'continued his operations upon as large a scale, it will be the noblest as well as the most extensive place in the Kingdom'.[22] And George Tate in the next century said that, on Brown's orders, 'the tops of the hills were planted with clumps of trees: other clumps mostly of a circular form were scattered over the slopes, and in other parts were long belts of plantations, while in the valleys larger forests were created... Greatly beautified and enriched was the scenery by these improvements'.[23]

Some two miles north-west of the castle, on another part of the estate in a remote

38. Watts's 1783 engraving of Alnwick Castle, Northumberland, from the north.

but splendid forest setting, perched on a bluff above an upper reach of the Aln stood the extensive ruins of the Carmelite priory of Hulne, enclosed by a tall stone wall. At the centre of this complex the Duke used the stones of the ruins to have built a delightful two storey Gothic summer house. Adam undoubtedly designed the interior, but the details of the exterior, which closely resemble those of the bath house at Corsham, suggest that this was Brown's design. The setting helps to make it one of the most delightful of his small buildings,

In 1772 the Alnwick Castle Archives record the following small payment: 'For a postchaise to Hampton Court to Mr Brown about a man to conduct the works at Alnwick on the death of Mr Griffin. Postillion and Turnpike. 0 – 18 – 0'. Cornelius Griffin had been Brown's foreman at several other places.[24] Working as Brown did on projects spread so widely about the country, he relied on the loyalty and competence of the men he put in charge of each of them. He repaid them with consideration. Writing from Northumberland House on 26 July, the Duke's steward says he understands that Mr Brown will 'take some care' of Griffin's widow when she arrives with friends in London. Meanwhile the Duke was abroad and this may explain why it was over a month before the postchaise was sent to Hampton. By then a 'man to conduct the work at Alnwick' must have been needed urgently.

Long before this, Brown had been at work at Syon House, the Duke's property

39. Syon House at Brentford.

which stood close to the Thames, facing on the other side the royal palace of Richmond. Direct evidence for what Brown did here is scarce — no plans or contracts survive. Canaletto also painted Syon, and if he recorded accurately what he saw, its large formal terrace surrounded by red brick walls had already gone by 1750. Brown's earliest payments from the Duke were made in 1754 and 1755, and it is then that he probably contributed his share in naturalizing the whole area between the house and the Thames. By 1761 'a fine lawn extending from Isleworth to Brentford' had been created. 'By these means also a beautiful prospect is opened into the king's gardens at Richmond, as well as up and down the Thames... In consequence... even the Thames itself seems to belong to the gardens, and the different sorts of vessels which successively sail as it were through them, appear to be the property of their noble proprietor...'

The gardens had also been extended to the north, the old part divided from the new by a serpentine river. 'It communicates with the Thames, is well stored with all sorts of river fish, and can be emptied and filled by means of a sluice.'[25] Lake and water meadows survive little changed today.

George III may well have looked across the Thames from Richmond, seen Brown's improvements at Syon and been finally persuaded that he should employ him. Whatever the explanation, the *Gentleman's Magazine* of July 1764 announced a royal appointment for Brown, though it got the precise name of his position wrong. As the royal warrant of the following March confirmed, he had in fact been made Chief Gardener (more commonly called Master Gardener) at Hampton Court.[26]

Brown had finally achieved the recognition which for the past five years, in spite of the support of so many rich and powerful clients, he had frustratingly been denied.

His payment for the job was to be £1107 6s, plus extra sums of £100 for growing pineapples and £100 for growing forced fruits for the royal family. Next year, St James's Park was added to his responsibilities for an additional salary of £40.[27] In practice, he was paid £2000 a year for the rest of his life, in quarterly instalments of £500.[28] As one of his letters explains (see overleaf), he had to spend a proportion of this on workmen, trees and plants, but it was nevertheless a useful regular income.

By now he had a general assistant in his private practice (as opposed to head men for particular projects). In April 1764 (see page 108) he had left John Spyers at Tottenham Park in Wiltshire, to make a twenty-four day survey of the grounds, on which to base his own proposals. This was a pattern which repeated itself at many places. Spyers's surviving plans show that he was a competent draftsman, and five years later when Brown had become Lord of the Manor of Fenstanton he employed Spyers to make a folio of elegant plans of his new estate.[29]

Spyers lived at Hampton — either a coincidence, or a suggestion that Brown knew of his royal appointment before it was made public. So did Brown's other new assistant, Samuel Lapidge. Both Spyers and Lapidge remained with Brown for the rest of his life, and Lapidge acted as his executor and completed some of his commissions.

The Browns also moved from Hammersmith to Hampton, where they were given the use of a building in the palace grounds known as Wilderness House. Here Brown lived for the rest of his life. Even when, in 1768, he bought Fenstanton Manor, he continued to consider Wilderness House his main residence and the following year, 1769, applied for additional buildings there at a cost of £474. Later that year he asked for another £20 10s to have a cellar made under his new room instead of a kitchen, and a brew-house turned into a kitchen. Although this was agreed, in January 1773 he wrote to the treasury complaining about persistent flooding, suggesting that his kitchen had not in fact been moved. Again he was granted permission to build a new one.[30]

Wilderness House stands today, a solid brick house of the late seventeenth century, its central part little changed. In Brown's time its front door faced Richmond Road, down which he would drive to Richmond Park. Today the house faces in the opposite direction, onto a long, narrow, half-walled garden at the end of which stands Wilderness Cottage, possibly once Brown's coach house. An attic window of the main house still looks down on the famous maze which lies close by. On the ground floor are the four small but elegant panelled rooms, in one of which he must often have worked and drawn by candlelight. Below again are the well-built brick cellars which were once his kitchen and which still flood.

Brown made no important changes to the gardens at Hampton Court. According to tradition, 'on being solicited by the King to improve the grounds... he declined the hopeless task, out of respect to himself and his profession.'[31] He did however, probably replace the terrace steps in the Privy Garden with gravel and grass slopes 'because we ought not to go up and down stairs in the open air'.[32]

And he clearly took his fruit-growing responsibilities seriously. The year after he arrived he was asking for garden pots, bell glasses and orange tubs; in 1772 for forcing frames to be 'put in order and a new stove made for raising pineaples and to fit up part of the old one for raising strawberrys and cherrys'; and in 1773 for 'a brick frame for raising mellons after the Dutch manner'.[33]

Furthermore, in 1768 he planted the Great Vine at Hampton Court, a Black Hamburg, from a cutting taken at Valentines, Ilford, Essex. By 1855 'its branches extended over a space of 2,300 square feet' and it was 'generally bearing upwards of 2,000 bunches'.[34] In the nineteenth century it was believed to flourish because its roots had made their way into the vast drains of the palace, but E. Law, Victorian historian of Hampton Court suggested instead that they probably reached 60 feet to the river bed.[35] Today its roots are nourished by the manuring of a large plot to one side of its glasshouse which is kept unplanted.

But it can hardly have been Brown's fruit-growing preoccupations, and was more probably his private practice, or perhaps a lack of enthusiasm for acting as housekeeper to a formal garden, which led to his being accused in 1769 of neglecting Hampton Court. In July of that year the Board of Works had the gardens surveyed and in October wrote to tell him that they were not being 'kept agreeable to the tenor of his contract therefore desire he would without loss of time put them in a proper condition'. The survey had reported that 'none of the Walkes [were] fit for use, and most of the other parts of the gardens much neglected'. In December the Lords of the Treasury also wrote to Brown.[36]

In reply he defended himself angrily:

... I believe if any body had a right to have censured my conduct it was the Surveyor of the gardens, which would have been very agreeable to me, because I know the gardens are in exceeding good order, and I can assure you that I lay out an hundred pounds a year more than my predecessor did, my wish and my intention is to keep them better and to put them in better order than ever I saw them in, and have stopped at no expense in procuring trees and plants, nor grudged any number of hands that were necessary. I this day went through the gardens, and my foreman told me they had more hands than they knew how to employ. But you Sir have only done your duty. You will be so good as to inform the gentlemen of the Board of Works that pique I pity, that ideal power I laugh at, that the insolence of office I despise, and that real power I will ever disarm by doing my duty.

Your obedient servant
Lancelot Brown

P.S. The gravel at H: Court is totally worn out; I have been obliged in the course of this year to break it up three times, otherwise it would have been green grass.[37]

Now that he was a royal gardener, Brown would have been much aware of the man who was to become his fiercest critic, William Chambers. Chambers, first as one of the two Architects of the Works, then from 1769 as Comptroller of the Works, was a regular member of the Board of Works and was present at all those meetings which considered Brown's applications for improvements to his house or for gardening equipment at Hampton Court, and at those at which the criticism of his work was discussed.

Chambers was seven years younger than Brown, the son of a Scottish merchant, born in Gothenburg, Sweden, but educated at Ripon, Yorkshire. In due course, as the architect of Buckingham House and Somerset House, as the Treasurer of the Royal Academy and as Surveyor General and Comptroller of the Board of Works, he became almost as well known as Brown, but his own description of his relationships with his clients shows that these were of a very different kind from the friendly and lasting ones which Brown so often enjoyed. In 1772 he wrote to his friend, the Revd Weston of Witney: 'I shall enter your door with a jovial heart, which I seldom have in the mansions of the great. With you I shall consider myself as a welcome guest. With them I am like the Egiptian bird who picks the teeth of the crocadile, admitted and cherished while there is work to be done, but when that is over the doors are shut and the farce is at an end'.[38]

As a young man Chambers had made three voyages to the Far East, which were to have an important influence on his work. Then in 1749 he was patronized by Frederick, Prince of Wales, who had been holding court at Kew for the previous twenty years. Chambers submitted plans for the House of Confucius, and for the Alhambra for Kew's gardens.[39] When the prince died in 1751 he prepared plans for a mausoleum, also to be built at Kew, though it never was.

Six years later Chambers was appointed architectural tutor to the new Prince of Wales, the future George III, and architect to Frederick's widow, Princess Augusta, who now planned to continue her late husband's improvements at Kew. The grounds here had previously been a small appendage to the palace. Now Chambers greatly extended them, to make an elongated area stretching the whole length of the present Botanic Gardens, but nowhere except at the palace itself fronting the river. The gardens he created here owed nothing to Brown's influence, but derived their inspiration from the pleasure gardens which Kent had been designing in the 1730s. They had no distant vistas or serpentine waters but looked inwards, if they looked anywhere, to two lawns enclosed by ha-has. Like Kent's gardens, they were designed to be perambulated, each stage revealing a new temple or ruin, each intended to arouse a particular emotion. In comparison with most Brown gardens they remained small, even when Chambers had elongated them, but by 1763 contained some thirty temples and other ornaments, including Chambers's well-known Chinese pagoda.

Meanwhile, running alongside Kew Palace's gardens, between them and the river, lay the grounds of Richmond Palace. John Roque's map of 1748 shows the Palace surrounded by formal gardens including a canal, a mount, gravel walks, lawns and a 'wild chestnut' avenue. More distantly there was a deer park in one direction, two wildernesses in another and woods in a third. In these last stood Kent's hermitage and his Merlin's Cave, that strange fantasy once kept by the rustic poet, clergyman and Queen's favourite, Stephen Duck. Interwoven with all these were meadows and cornfields. Much of this land now forms the riverside section of the Botanic Gardens, though the site of the palace itself lies beyond, on a golf course.

Until Princess Augusta died in 1772 and left Kew Palace vacant, the King took a far keener interest in Richmond and its grounds than he did in Kew, and as soon as Brown arrived at Hampton Court he commissioned him to transform them. These were the gardens which looked across the Thames to Syon, and the King may well have wanted a similar transformation to that which he had seen Brown produce there. Certainly Brown's plan of 1764 proposed this.[40] Every formal feature was to be eliminated. The area between the palace and the river was to be transformed into lawn, set with individual trees and clumps. Elsewhere a number of curving drives were to approach the palace from behind, or wind away towards Kew.

The destructive part of this work was undoubtedly carried out, and though both the Hermitage and Merlin's Cave are named on Brown's plan, they probably went too. On 11 October 1765 the Board of Works noted a report by Joshua Kirby, Clerk of the Works at Richmond, 'that great alterations and improvements were making in Richmond Gardens by Mr Launcelot Browne and that for some time he is to take care of that part of the garden where the said alterations are making and whether Mr Havefirle should be paid his whole allowance for taking care of Richmond Gardens, notwithstanding his having nothing to do for the present with that part of the gardens where the alternations are making'.[41]

The constructive part of the work was the unification of the whole area into one great park. As so often, it meant turning arable land into woodland or grazing, and Thomas Richardson's map of 1771 shows that this had been done. In one sense therefore, the parts of Richmond which today form the riverside section of Kew are Brown's work. Specifically, the sunken Rhododendron Walk is probably his since it corresponds with one of the driveways which his plan shows. The lake is not his — it was made in 1856-61 — but close to its eastern end there still stands what is almost certainly the 'Large Oak' named on his plan.

A letter from one of Brown's workmen confirms the King's interest in the work at Richmond. It describes an unexpected afternoon visit by the King and Queen, after Brown had gone home for the day. 'I told the King you stayed till two o'clock and that I had said to you that their Majestys seldom ever came after that time. He said he had been detained but should see you next Saturday... He was much pleased with the levels and asked if you was not so too. I told him you found no faults.'[42]

The letters of John Milliken, the young man whom Brown had employed as his assistant at Richmond, confirm that from the start the King and Queen were keenly interested in the work. To his wife Milliken wrote: 'The King and Queen

40. The Rhododendron Walk at Kew Gardens.

come 2 or 3 days a week here and talkes as free and I think is as bent on the work as ever the Duke of Devonshire was'.

Brown was particularly attached to Milliken. He had brought him from Chats worth — hence Milliken's reference to the Duke of Devonshire — but told him first to 'do all the good you can whilst you remain at Chatsworth, because for the sake of the great good man that is you'. At Richmond, according to Milliken, Brown paid him more than he had ever paid anyone before, but told him not to put this in his accounts in case it 'would raise a murmuring amongst his other men'. Until Milliken could bring his wife Polly south to join him and employ a servant Brown provided him with one of his own old ones, who 'takes good care of my shoes, boots etc. makes my fire and go erands'.[43]

The fact that Milliken lived at Kew and worked for Brown till Brown's death (and for the King for seventeen years more) suggests that in practice Brown continued to have charge of Richmond, and probably of Kew as well after 1772. At Richmond he was in still closer contact with Chambers. While Brown was landscaping, Chambers was surrounding the King's house there with various garden buildings, including the Observatory and a fete pavilion, and preparing four separate schemes, none of them carried out, for building a new palace. It has often been said that Chambers's hostility to Brown was the result of Brown's plan, not Chambers's being selected by Clive of India for his new house at Claremont, near Esher, but it seems likely that Chambers already disapproved of Brown's work, as a result of his first-hand experience of it at Richmond.

7. The Excellence of Blenheim

'LE BRUN', wrote the philosopher Rochefoucauld, had so quick and sure an eye for country that after riding round it for half an hour he would conceive the design for a whole park, and that afterwards half a day sufficed for him to mark it out on the ground.[1] It is interesting to compare this often quoted comment with the history of Brown's work at Tottenham Park in Wiltshire where, at about the same time that he received his royal appointment at Hampton Court, he began to work for Lord Bruce, twenty-first hereditary warden of Savernake. This great mediaeval forest, which had once included a hundred square miles of countryside south of Marlborough, was still large. Tottenham Park lay towards its southern end. Here an earlier Elizabethan house had been burned down, and in its place Lord Bruce's uncle, the Third Earl of Ailesbury, had had designed and built for him by Lord Burlington in the 1720s a fine red brick mansion.

Bruce had inherited Tottenham in 1747, when he was only seventeen. He was the youngest of four brothers, and had been chosen by his uncle as the nephew least likely to inherit some additional great estate which might interest him more. He grew up a correct and, judging by his letters, somewhat fussy man, who did not disappoint his uncle. In the 1750s he had already begun to plant in Savernake Forest, and though for many years he dabbled in politics, becoming a Lord of the Bedchamber to George III and later Governor to the future George IV, throughout his time at court he remained keenly concerned with his Wiltshire estate, and in 1776 temporarily retired there. According to Thackeray he did this in pique because he had been put right by the young Prince when he 'made a false quantity in quoting Greek'.[2] Letters from Bruce's wife, complaining that his court duties were depriving her of 'so many *peaceful* domestic joys' and leaving her in sole charge of her four children are a more probable explanation.[3]

She was Susanna Hoare, daughter of the banker, Henry Hoare, who for the previous fifteen years had been transforming ninety acres of Wiltshire thirty miles to the south-west of Savernake at Stourhead into the finest of all eighteenth century landscape gardens. Bruce was probably encouraged by his wife to improve his own grounds, and his father-in-law certainly took an interest. Among the Ailesbury

41. Blenheim Palace, Oxfordshire.

papers there is a red chalk sketch of Tottenham House, with a pencil plan of the forest on its back, which was found with a slip of paper that clearly refers to the plan and reads: 'Sketch by Mr Hoare of what he understands to be Mr Brown's idea for improvements in the forest so as to make it one great whole'.[4]

The plan is not dated, but can have been made at the earliest in the summer of 1764, by which time Brown had visited Tottenham. He was first there in March, and left his assistant, Spyers, who had spent the next twenty-four days surveying the estate. Even then Brown does not seem to have been able to meet Bruce. Since April of the previous year he had been trying to do so, and he continued to try for another year, writing letters which were always respectful but in the end less than usually patient.

On 6 March 1765 he wrote: 'It is a real mortification to me that I shall not be able to see your Lordship and Lady Bruce at Tottenham Park you were the objects of my western expedition... I shall however come there as soon as I can. I will then make Winckles [Bruce's bailiff] Master of the work. I removed the man that is there.'[5]

Bruce must have offered Brown a date but at the last minute cancelled it because two weeks later Brown wrote again:

I... am sorry to find that your Lordship has fixed on so early a day for leaving Tottenham Park. I am obliged to go to Blenheim for Wednesday or Thursday and I must go round by Lord Coventry and by Mr William Codringtons, which will take me up at least eight or ten Days. I wish your Lordship could stay a few days longer in the country or be a few days longer before you go. I have been calculating my time entirely for your Lordship and it will be an extreme mortification to me not to meet your Lordship. I beg your Lordship will contrive as much about this matter as possible because I have been contriving to make everybody meet me at their respective places which puts it out of my power to alter my rout. I fully intended to have waited on your Lordship tomorrow.[6]

In his letters Brown frequently enquires about Lady Bruce's health and sometimes it was this which forced him to postpone a visit to Tottenham. Just how much of an invalid Lady Bruce was, it is hard to be sure. A few years later (16 October 1772) Brown wrote: 'I am very sorry to hear Lady Bruce has been so much out of order, but I hope it will come to a happy conclusion very soon as I understand it is a disorder of the nine month sort'.[7] It was. The baby was born early the next year and Bruce wrote to his steward ordering a new clump of trees to be planted in honour of his new son Charles.

Brown's letters of March 1765 were the last concerned with trying to meet Bruce. Five months later he was writing on a different subject. If Brown found Bruce irritatingly difficult to contact, Bruce was equally irritated by Brown's failure to send his bills. On 26 August 1765 Brown wrote:

I am very much obliged to your Lordship for the venison, which arrived in perfect order and very good... I have been hurried beyond measure, of late...

Mr Bill [Bruce's agent, Charles Bill] has twice hinted to me that your Lordship wishes to have my account. All I can say on that matter is that I should be extremely sorry to make any demand that is not very agreeable to your Lordship; for my journeys and plan, the admeasurement of the ground I suppose one hundred and ten pounds, but I shall be very happy if your Lordship will satisfy yourself.[8]

A month later (21 September 1765) he explained himself more fully:

I am now in Staffordshire where I was honoured with your Lordship's letter I believe ten days ago or more, but I have been so much out of order that I have not been able to write nor do anything else. I sent up to my clerk to know what the demand was upon your Lordship which I did not know exactly by the book. He writes me word that the surveying and maping bill with the man's expenses at 6d per acre comes to near twenty-five pounds and as to my journeys and plans I have no fixed rule about it nor is it possible to do it but to charge less or more according to the size and trouble. All I can say upon it is that I should be very sorry to diminish my friends, and very sorry to increase my business, for I have so much to do that it neither answers for profit nor pleasure, for when I am galloping in one part of the world my men are making blunders and neglects which [make] it very unpleasant.

Of one thing I can assure your Lordship that if I can be of use to your Lordship I shall be very happy and as to money matters your Lordship will satisfy me when your Lordship is pleas'd.[9]

This is only one of several occasions on which Brown told his clients to pay him what they consider right. Such offers are a remarkable contrast to the letter which the garden designer Richard Woods wrote to Lord Arundell (see below), pleading for more than a guinea a day or he would be out of pocket. They make Brown's disagreements with Sir John Griffin two years later the harder to understand. In general they suggest that for Brown, if money was partly important in itself, it was equally important as a mark of approval. Such a need for reassurance might well be expected in a boy who had been taken from his own family and more or less adopted by a family of a higher class, then by the whole of that class.

Three weeks later Brown wrote to thank Bruce for a payment made to him at Drummonds Bank — and to say he was 'sorry to hear such a disagreeable account of Lady Bruce'.[10]

Another sixteen months passed (and a total of almost three years since Spyers's survey) before, on 12 February 1767, Brown wrote to Bruce saying that the plan for Tottenham Park was nearly finished.[11] Once again work had apparently begun months if not years before a plan was finally drawn.

Brown's later visits to Tottenham are more fully described than those to any other place. He came again in March and December 1765, in May, July and September 1766, in March, July and November 1767, in March 1768 and in January 1769. Even in the 1760s these may not have been the full number of visits, and he made others in the 1770s. On most of them careful memoranda were kept, either by Bruce's bailiff Winckles, or by his agent Bill, of the decisions he took. These memoranda would run to as many as seven closely written foolscap pages. For other visits lists of questions were prepared by Winckles or Bill and Brown's answers carefully written alongside.[12]

Though there is no reason to suggest that Brown worked differently elsewhere, at Tottenham Bruce seems to have encouraged such regular and careful supervision, either because he was precise by nature or because his absences in London made him anxious. On 16 February 1773, by which time most of the work had been completed, he wrote to his bailiff, Winckles, to warn him of another visit from Brown, and tell him to 'have all your questions wrote down and send me them and his answers'.[13]

Next day he wrote to Bill, telling him to make sure that Winckles recollected and minuted Brown's comments, and the day after again wrote to Winckles. 'When Brown makes you his visit this week I hope he will find the London Walk gates open, and the bed over your room well aired and that you will write down all his answers to the inclosed queries, besides other points I have repeatedly desired you to ask him about.'[14] And a week later he wrote to Winckles for the third time: 'You must endeavour to recollect exactly where he went with you and what he observed upon every spot, that I may know if possible every circumstance he took notice of besides answering the questions I directed you to put to him'.

Brown would give instructions and advice of the most detailed sort. When he found that 'Lady Bruce's peep from the large study window' was 'a straight line through a perfect avenue' he 'directed the cure of it by rounding off the plantation of laurels at the entrance of it on the left hand.' There was a fine beech there and Brown 'directed the scrub trees to be cleared away a little from behind it which would also enlarge the entrance to the narrow avenue'.[15]

When the dam of the pleasure garden's canal leaked, he recommended: 'To stop the leak in the lower canal a trench to be cut across the head at the south east, and a wall of clay rammed in'. When he toured the orchards he observed that the gardener, Edwards, 'has not the least notion in the world of pruning a fruit tree'.[16]

More generally Bill would record that 'Mr Brown advises forest trees particularly oaks to be scattered amongst the plantations, and even where they are intended to be ever-green clumps or plantations he would have a few oaks thinly scattered, observing that the oaks will be there when the evergreens are dead and gone'.[17]

At least Bill could be trusted to give full accounts of Brown's tours of inspection. 'Mr Brown came here on Sunday to dinner', he wrote, after Brown's second visit.

In the afternoon he took a view of the gardens in a storm of snow. Early this morning, which proved tolerably favourable, he allowed lining out and finally settled the serpentine walk all round the garden, marked such trees as were proper to be taken away and gave general directions to Winckles upon everything that occur'd. He thinks it best to keep Howse a fortnight or three weeks longer to get the levelling business forward. In general he approves of what has

42. Characteristic paired clumps of trees at Tottenham, Wiltshire.

been done except the taking away a few large trees in one or two places. If the high bank and trees had been taken down, great would have been the fall indeed, Brown would have excommunicated us all...[18]

In December the same year (1765) Brown, according to Bill, 'spoke much in commendation of shady rides as so frequently agreeable both in summer and winter, a fence both against heat and cold... Mr Brown thinks there is great capability about the Loggia and Octagon buildings, and he drop't us, he said, these few hints because he considered himself mortal... He seems very fond of leaving large clumps made upon the downs at a distance...'[19]

The essential features of Tottenham as Brown found it in 1764 are shown on a large painting now at Savernake Lodge, by a none-too-skilful, perhaps local artist. A carriage, traditionally said in the family to be George III's, is driving up an avenue of youngish trees towards Burlington's brick house, which stands at the top of a slight rise. In the right foreground at the end of woodland ridges are the Loggia and the Octagon — also built by Burlington.

On either side of the house are two rectangular ponds, and to its rear a long vegetable garden and a pleasure garden, both curiously tilted by the painter to show their layouts. Tottenham never had the massed seventeenth-century parterres which Brown so often discovered around his clients' houses and so ruthlessly removed. The estate's other great feature, the Grand Avenue, a three-and-a-half mile avenue of oaks and beeches which led north as far as the Bath road, began a little to one side of the house and as a result remained a forest rather than a garden feature.

Much of Brown's work was concerned with the pleasure garden, today tangled woodland. The rectangular ponds were filled, the vegetable garden moved to the other side of the house and a ha-ha built to the south — away from the main forest. Around the Octagon (which survives) and the Loggia (which doesn't) the woodland was much thinned. But today it is the large clumps which, as Bill reported, Brown was so fond of, that are the most impressive surviving feature of his work. They are double clumps, stretching away in pairs on either side of two avenues; the first the one up which George III was aproaching in the painting, leading today to the column which Bruce erected in the King's honour; the second leading towards the Grand Avenue, as if intended to join it at a fine angle. Some now consist of massive ancient trees, others have been faithfully replanted, though omitting the single copper beech which Brown planted at their centres. Where today they are engulfed by the forest, the tops of the older clumps rise above the young trees around them.

As for the forest itself, this had consisted of a number of mediaeval coppice woods, separated by wide grazing areas. According to Henry Hoare's pencil plan, the way in which Brown intended to make them one great whole was to create several looping rides which would have entirely ignored this mediaeval structure. More faintly shown on the plan is a suggestion of the much more conservative changes which Brown probably made: he planted the grazing areas with oak, leaving only narrow rides along them. The result is a geometrical pattern which has little connection either with Hoare's sketch or with Brown's usual serpentine woodland drives.

As a whole, Brown's connections with Tottenham show that Rochefoucauld's description of his methods could hardly be more inaccurate. Far from viewing the grounds in half an hour he left his man to make a survey of them which took him three and a half weeks, and the process of staking out the work took not half a day but years. Later writers about Brown have, perhaps unfairly, drawn the further implication that a single visit completed Brown's part in the operation, which he left to others to carry out in his absence. If Tottenham is typical, the exact opposite is true. He made visit after visit, adjusting detail after detail.

'I am on my way to Blenheim,' Brown wrote to Bruce in March 1765.[20] He had begun to work at Blenheim at about the same time that he was first trying to meet Bruce at Tottenham. Of all Brown's landscapes, Blenheim is most often admired.

XVI. Lancelot 'Capability' Brown by Richard Cosway.

XVII. (Overleaf) The view along the side of Vanbrugh's part-flooded bridge to Blenheim Palace in the distance.

XVIII. Twilight on the lake at Blenheim, Oxfordshire.

XIX. Brilliant autumn colour at Blenheim.

43. Brown grassed over Henry Wise's State Garden to the south of Blenheim Palace, but formal gardens beside the building were re-introduced earlier this century. The water parterre shown above is on the west side.

But admiration is often tinged with regret because of a notion that although what he did here was splendid, he destroyed in the process things by Wise and Vanburgh which had been equally fine. Those who knew Blenheim before Brown came would not have agreed. About Vanburgh's Grand Bridge, Horace Walpole wrote that it 'begs for a drop of water and is refused'.[21] Of the park as a whole the First Duchess of Marlborough said, ''tis a chaos which only God Almighty could finish'.[22] The Duchess had been dead for almost twenty years before Brown arrived to play this role.

Then, in 1764, George Spencer, Fourth Duke of Marlborough, was twenty-five years old. He was red-green colour blind. 'It is certain,' Horace Walpole wrote, 'that the present Duke of Marlborough and his brother Lord Robert Spencer have very imperfect discrimination of colours, especially of scarlet and green, which both have called, though those colours are so unlike, the alternative of what they are — till having been so often questioned and teased on that subject, neither cares to speak of it.'[23]

44. Engraving of *A North West View of Blenheim House and Park in The County of Oxford*. 1752.

The Duke was anyway a shy man, but played *quinze* 'uncommonly well. He told Sir J. Reynolds one day... that having made a master-stroke at that game by which he should have made a hundred pounds, he put his cards into a heap and lost what he had set on them, knowing that if he had shown them, which it was necessary to do to win the money, all the company at the different tables would have come round him, and the fineness of the stroke would have been their topic for half an hour. This he acknowledged he could not stand.'[24]

By the time Brown had been working for the Duke for nine years and achieved his great design at Blenheim, he seems occasionally to have taken advantage of the Duke's shyness. Horace Walpole told Lady Ossory of his 'impertinence to the Duke of Marlborough', commenting: 'The moment a fashionable artist, singer or actor is insolent, his success is sure. The first peer that experiences it, laughs to conceal his being angry, the next flatters him for fear of being treated familiarly, and ten more bear it because it is *so like Brown*'.[25]

At Blenheim the Duke's grounds contained interesting enough features, but they were widely separated and seemed unrelated. Vanburgh's great, sand-coloured palace stood high up on one side of the valley of the little river Glyme — the same river that Brown had dammed at Kiddington when he first came south. To cross the valley Vanburgh's bridge needed to be grand, and though Walpole was not strictly accurate in saying the bridge was waterless, the Glyme would have been dwarfed by its size, even if it had not been made into a straight-sided canal. North of the bridge there was a gap before the Grand Avenue started near the Column of Victory; and the avenue then rapidly passed over the brow of the hill so that most of its two miles was out of sight. The Great Park through which it ran was dotted here and there with geometric clumps of trees but they had no particular pattern.

East of the palace, there was a second, much shorter avenue, and south-east of this an area of woodland, criss-crossed by a regular pattern of rides, known as the Lower Park. Directly south of the palace was the huge hexagonal parterre laid out by Wise in the early 1700s. To its south-west were ancient oak woods. Perhaps it was Blenheim's sheer size (2,500 acres) which seemed to separate these features and make the First Duchess consider it needed God's help. Brown's inspiration was to create an even more dramatic feature, a great lake, which would be sufficiently dominating to make other features (both those he left and his new plantations) seem related to each other. When the idea first occurred to him he may well have felt it impossible because, to make the lake of sufficient size, he needed to flood Vanburgh's bridge to its waist. His second thought must then have been, why not?

Brown probably made his plan for Blenheim in 1764, and at the same time sketched his idea for the Grand Cascade which was to form part of the lake's dam — plan and sketch both survive. His plan included a second dam and cascade, lower down the Glyme close to the point where it leaves the grounds, and the creating here of a meandering artificial river; the planting of a peripheral belt of trees round the Great Park and of carefully placed trees and clumps, one as large as 14 acres, around the new waters; and the total removing of Wise's parterre.

The lake was unfinished when, in about 1769, Thomas Whately visited Blenheim, but already he could judge its effect.

> In front of Blenheim was a deep broad valley, which abruptly separated the castle from the lawn and the plantations before it; even a direct approach could not be made, without building a monstrous bridge over this vast hollow: but the forced communication was only a subject of raillery, and the scene continued broken into two parts, absolutely distinct from each other. This valley has been lately flooded; it is not filled; the bottom only is covered with water; the sides are still very high, but they are no longer the steeps of a chasm; they are the bold shores of a noble river.

After describing the plantations around this new river, Whately continues, 'and the river in its long varied course, approaching to every object, and touching upon every part, spreads its influence over the whole. Notwithstanding their distances from each other, they all seem to be assembled about the water'.[26]

Though Brown's achievement at Blenheim was admired from his own time onwards, some of his techniques have only been analysed and recognized during the last few years. These discoveries make what he did seem even more remarkable. The most interesting are concerned with his water works, and with his tree planting.

For example, knowing exactly to what level he needed to flood the Grand Bridge, he was able to build the Grand Cascade to precisely the correct height though the two were out of sight of each other even before the woodland which now separates them had become so dense. Still more interesting, the long curving course which the new water follows below the Great Cascade, which at first seems natural, is not. Brown raised this downstream length above the Glyme's natural bed and led it along a side-cut canal which he built some 30 yards up the valley's side. Only three or four years after the completion of the first English commercial canal (the Bridgewater to Manchester in 1761) Brown apparently understood the techniques of canal building and had the confidence to use them. It seems, as I have suggested, a fair guess to connect this understanding and confidence with his association since 1759 with the Duke of Bridgewater, 'Father of Inland Waterways'. Certainly Brown continued to know Bridgewater, and describes meeting him in a letter to the Earl of Bute in 1767.[27]

As for Brown's planting at Blenheim, this has now been examined with a thoroughness that has not been applied before, either to his work here or, as far as I know, to any of his planting elsewhere. The landscape architect who was consulted[28] took twelve points on the carriage drives north of the palace and by drawing out the view lines which these gave was able to show how precisely Brown planted. In place after place one extra tree would have blocked a view of lake, palace or garden feature.

William Mavor, the rector of Woodstock, in his *A New Description of Blenheim*, 1789, confirmed the effects this produced. 'The Water, the Palace, the Gardens, the Pillar, Woodstock, and other near and remote objects, open and shut upon the eye like enchantment; and at one point, every change of a few paces furnishes a new scene, each of which would form a subject worthy of the sublimest pencil.' Mavor had an instinctive understanding of Brown's method. 'Because Brown could execute better than he could describe, and worked by self-taught rules, he has been attacked with unbecoming asperity; and some of his most capital performances have been ascribed to chance.'[29]

Later commentators, even if they haven't ascribed Brown's results to chance, have suggested that his genius was of an inspirational kind. The evidence about the way he worked at Tottenham, returning again and again to make small but vital adjustments to his plantings till he got precisely the effects he wanted, is supported by an analysis of the effects of his planting at Blenheim. The more his work is examined the better evidence it provides for Blake's opinion that 'Mechanical excellence is the only vehicle of genius'.[30]

It is another aspect of his planting at Blenheim which now seems to show an insight close to inspiration. He apparently had an uncannily accurate idea of how his trees would mature. Though over two hundred years have passed, those which survive still frame and do not interrupt Blenheim's splendid vistas.

45. Blenheim Palace from the air. (Aerofilms Ltd.)

Perhaps Brown was unduly pleased with his achievement. His familiarity with the Duke suggests that this was a period when he was less than usually modest. It is interesting that this was also the time of his quarrel with Sir John Griffin of Audley End; and it can hardly be a coincidence that at this time, probably in April 1765, he informed his bank that he was no longer to be known as Mr Lancelot Brown, but in future as Lancelot Brown Esq.[31] Certainly it was when surveying Blenheim's great new water that he made his most quoted remark, used by some diarists of the day as evidence of conceit. Joseph Cradock was kinder:

I was at Hampton Green for some time with Mr Brown, who seemed to have a confirmed asthma. He generally walked about in the grounds during dinner time. I found him to be a most agreeable unassuming man; and I said to Mr Bates, 'I cannot recognise an atom of the Capability Brown I have heard so much talk of'... I mentioned to my friend, that I could trace nothing of the alleged presumption of saying, after he had finished the water at Blenheim, 'Thames, Thames wilt never forgive me'.

And it was John Byng, usually a grouchy commentator, who surely caught most accurately the flavour of Brown's remark when he wrote that it was made with Brown's 'usual pompous drollery'.[32]

8. Lord of the Manor

 THE MID 1760s were Brown's busiest years. In 1763 or 1764, besides those commissions already described, he began work in the south of the country at Broadlands in Hampshire; in London at Wimbledon Park; in the home counties at Wrotham Park, Hertfordshire, Luton Hoo, Bedfordshire, and Navestock, Essex; in East Anglia at Redgrave, Suffolk, and Melton Constable, Norfolk; in the Midlands at Stoke Park, Buckinghamshire, and Fawsley, Northamptonshire; in the west at Dodington, Gloucestershire, and Prior Park, Somerset, and in the far north at Lowther, Westmorland.

Next year, 1765, came Compton Wynyates in Warwickshire, Tong Castle in Shropshire, Eldon in Suffolk, Upper Gatton in Surrey, and around this time, Rothley in his native county of Northumberland.

When Brown had walked to school from Kirkharle to Cambo he had passed Wallington House, the property of Sir Walter Calverley Blackett, and perhaps been impressed by the improvements to its grounds which Blackett was already making. According to tradition, Brown now, some twenty-five years later, gave Blackett advice at Wallington, but there is no evidence to support this suggestion, and Sir George Trevelyan, whose family later owned Wallington did not believe it. 'A master,' he wrote, 'or, more properly speaking, a despot, in the art of estate ornamentation — who spoiled, or improved, but at all events entirely transformed, many of the most famous parks and gardens in England... was never allowed to try his hand at Wallington for fear of his doctoring and deforming the natural features of the ground.'[1]

Nor is there much firm evidence that Brown now worked for Sir William Loraine, grandson of the Sir William who had first employed him at Kirkharle, apart from John Hodgson's claim that it was in the second Sir William's time that 'The magic hand of Brown contrived to throw the sweetest charms into the fields of the place of his nativity, and to convert the landscape around the mansion into a "woody theatre of stateliest view"'.[2]

Certainly the trees around Kirkharle estate suggest that they could have formed part of an encircling belt, and the newly found plan of Kirkharle would give

46. Coombe Abbey, near Coventry.

Hodgson some support if it dated from Brown's mature years, but not if, as I have suggested in the first chapter, it was drawn before he ever left Kirkharle.

Rothley is another matter. This was a detached part of Blackett's estate, lying some four miles north of his Wallington House. Five plans for improving Rothley survive.[3] From their style they are almost certainly Brown's, and Hodgson confirms that the lakes at Rothley were made under Brown's direction. They consist of two sheets of water, he added, 'one on each side of the Almouth Road: that on the east is in a winding dell, with steep banks on each side, partly covered with natural wood: the other is broader, much more extensive and hemmed in on each side with deep plantations of larch and pine'.[4]

Two of Brown's plans are of the lakes. One shows the narrow, eastern end of the upper lake. The other seems to be a detail of the same eastern tip, though it is surprisingly inscribed, 'A sketch of the head of the intended piece of water. NB. The earth to be taken away from the banks to give it this form and the head to be made 25 feet wide at the top'. Elsewhere Brown always uses the term 'head' to mean the dam of a lake, but here he seems to mean the end at which the Ewesley Burn entered, and the measurement he gives refers, not to the width of the top of a dam but to the width of the water.

Two castle-style follies were built on rocky outcrops nearby during Blackett's time — Rothley Castle, and Codger Fort — and Brown perhaps had a say in the siting of them, but he did not design them.[5]

In 1770 when the Revd Arthur Young passed by he found a 'fine newly made lake... surrounded by young plantations, which is noble water: the bends and curves of the bank are bold and natural, and when the trees get up, the whole spot

47. Undated plan of the eastern part of Rothley Lake, attributed to Brown. Wallington, Northumberland. (By courtesy of the National Trust.)

will be remarkably beautiful'.[6] The trees around the lower lake have now got up, and this secluded nature reserve is indeed remarkably beautiful, the more so because of the contrast it makes with the bleak surrounding moorland.

Brown was also working throughout these years for the Earl of Scarbrough at Sandbeck, Yorkshire, a commission which led to one of his stranger pieces of landscaping. The Scarbroughs' main home had previously been at Lumley Castle, in County Durham, but at Sandbeck in about 1765 the Fourth Earl began to build himself a fine new stone mansion to the design of James Paine, where he then resided.

Though Scarbrough was not an important politician, he took some part in the rapid shifts of power of the 1760s. He was twice Cofferer of the Household to George III, and from 1765 to 1777 Earl Marshal. According to Paine — who as his architect may have been prejudiced — he had great taste for the fine arts, particularly architecture and planting so that 'the natural beauties of this situation [Sandbeck's] could not possibly escape him'.[7]

The countryside around Sandbeck with its rolling cornfields, has been compared by Mark Girouard to northern France. 'Out of this rolling sea the Sandbeck woods rise like an island — an effect particularly prominent as one approaches it from Doncaster. For Sandbeck is almost entirely surrounded by woods or belts of trees, inside which it rules over its own secluded and peaceful landscape. To create this kind of private Elysium on the grand scale was one of the great achievements of Georgian England. It is an achievement inseparably bound up with the name of 'Capability' Brown.'[8] But although Brown was paid sums varying between £200 and £600 in each of the four years 1762 to 1766,[9] there is some mystery about precisely what he agreed to do at Sandbeck, for no contract survives.

The way in which he transformed the grounds, however, can be seen clearly from two plans which bracket this period, the first of 1724 by Joseph Dickinson, showing in front of the house a string of fish ponds and a large area of woodland with typical early eighteenth century diverging rides, the second of 1840 by R. Smith showing two large lakes at the back of the house, of which there was no sign before.

These lakes were almost certainly Brown's. The top one, of 14 acres, still forms the principal garden feature, now seen through a scattering of mature limes and chestnuts. The second survives too, hidden 30 feet lower beyond groves of willows, now fished by the local miners' angling club.

This was by no means the end of Brown's connection with Sandbeck. A mile away stood the romantic ruins of Roche Abbey, hemmed into the valley of a small tributary of the river Ryton by wooded slopes and walls of rock. As early as 1756 Lady Scarbrough had written that a fine piece of water could be made here, but 'this is among my Lord's last schemes... as it will be a great work to do'.[10] Sixteen years later nothing had been done and it was then that Horace Walpole wrote: 'I saw Roche Abbey too, which is hid in such a venerable chasm, that you might lie concealed there even from a squire-parson of the parish. Lord Scarbrough, to

48. The ruins of Roche Abbey near Sandbeck, Yorkshire.

whom it belongs, and who lives at next door, neglects it as much as if he was afraid of ghosts'.[11] It was not for another two years that Brown and the Earl drew up a five-clause contract. It included finishing the work around Sandbeck House and detailed the changes Brown was to make around 'Roach' Abbey.[12]

This contract is of particular interest because it commits Brown to improving the abbey 'with poet's feeling and with painter's eye', a quotation from the Reverend William Mason's recently published poem 'The English Garden'. Clearly Brown read his contemporaries, and was not above accepting their definitions of his aims.

Brown found the abbey ruins overgrown. His plan, which he put into effect during the next three years, cleared away the confusion, enlarged a nearby hammer pond (there had once been a forge here) into a lake, and gave this a cascade. Brown did more. He seems to have considered the many low fragments of the old abbey buildings a distraction, for he covered them over and sowed the resulting flat ground with grass and Dutch clover, leaving only the large upright portions showing.

William Gilpin, writing about the work when it was in progress, said:

This is the first subject of the kind he has attempted. Many a modern palace he has adorned and beautified: but a ruin presented a new idea, which I doubt whether he has sufficiently considered. He has finished one of the valleys... floated it with a lake and formed a very beautiful scene. But I fear it is too magnificent and too artificial an appendage to be in unison with the ruins of an abbey. An abbey it is true, may stand by the side of a lake; and it is possible that this lake may, in some future time, become its situation, when the marks of the spade and pick-axe are removed, when its osiers flourish, and its naked banks become fringed and covered with wood... The ruin now stands on a neat bowling green.[13]

The impression Gilpin gives, suggesting as it does one of today's sanitized Ministry of the Environment sites, is not confirmed by contemporary paintings, which show that Brown left many trees standing among the ruins, and that the effect was by no means bald.

Whatever Brown did, it was not appreciated by later Earls of Scarbrough. The present Earl remembers his father telling him that his enthusiasm for visits to Sandbeck during school holidays before the First World War was much qualified by his regularly being sent with his brother to help dig out the ruins of Roche Abbey which Brown had buried.

Today the re-exposed ruins seem to prove that Brown was wrong, but his lake and cascade add much to what remains a delightful, secluded valley (see page 133).

In 1767, while the early work at Sandbeck was still in progress, Brown was commissioned by the First Earl of Ashburnham to landscape his estate of Ashburnham near Battle in East Sussex. Nine years earlier, in 1758, the Earl had known enough of Brown's work or reputation to have been one of the fourteen who signed the petition on his behalf to obtain him a royal position. By then Ashburnham was certainly not short of money. In 1756 he had married Elizabeth Crowley, described by Walpole as 'one of the plump Crowleys'.[14] She was the daughter of a London alderman, and had brought him a small fortune of £200,000. Two years later Walpole had watched him (with other clients of Brown) paying absurd prices for paintings at Schaub's auction. 'In short, there was Sir James Lowther, Mr Spencer, Sir Richard Grosvenor, boys with 20 or £30,000 a year and the Duchess of Portland, Lord Ashburnham, Lord Egremont, and others with near as much, who care not what they give.'[15]

But Ashburnham had chosen to spend the first years after his marriage on rebuilding his house, not its grounds. Some of his energy had also gone into promoting himself as a courtier. As early as 1747, when he was only twenty-three, he had had made for himself 'a magnificent summer suit to wait' at court, but been disappointed when Lord Cowper failed to resign the Bedchamber.[16] Five years later he was one of six lords being considered for the position of Governor to the future George III and eagerly wishing for it,[17] but again he was disappointed. Next year he became Keeper of Hyde Park and Keeper of St James's Park, with a salary of £1,000, and in 1765 he was appointed to the Great Wardrobe.[18]

It was soon after this that he turned his attention to the grounds of Ashburnham. He was another of Brown's clients who must have needed careful handling. When his court career finally ended in 1782, after seven years as Groom of the Stole, he resigned 'in dudgeon and not very gracefully' because he had not been given the Garter.[19] And at an earlier time there had been a great quarrel 'between two very wise Lords, Lord Lyncon and Lord Ashburnham, which should have a French cook. No water language was ever worse than what passed between them'.[20] But once again Brown had an amicable and satisfactory relationship with his employer. Payments from Ashburnham arrived regularly in Brown's account at Drummonds Bank from 1767 to 1773, and for a second contract from 1774 to 1781.

In the earliest of these years, 1767, Brown drew for Ashburnham one of his largest plans, measuring 6½ feet by 4½ feet. It proposed numerous new features, including a kitchen garden, a melon ground with stoves, an ice house, a menagerie, a bridge and a Gothic back for some almshouses, but its central feature was a large 'intended water'. The house already looked over a shallow valley which held an 'old water'. Who made this is unknown. It was not there thirty years before. Brown's intended water began where the old water ended and stretched away to the south-west for a similar distance. The plan shows it as about the same width as the old water, but when it was actually made it was substantially wider, hence its present name, the Broad Water.

Beyond both waters the land rose fairly steeply and here Brown showed hanging woods. These already existed, probably consisting, as today, of eighty per cent oak. Ashburnham had been one of the royal forests of Sussex, and the Sussex iron industry, depending on charcoal, finally died out here. They were known as Burwash Wood and were divided by an elaborate, geometric pattern of rides. Brown's plan eliminated these rides, making the wood a single whole.

The work of building the dam for Brown's lake must have been enormous. It raised the head of the water some 50 feet above the level of the Grand Wish Brook. But it seems to have proceeded without difficulty. Not so the point at which the old lake ended and the new one began. Here Brown eventually constructed a so-called 'stocking' of water — an overlapping extension of the old water — which appears on a second plan to form exactly the shape of a leg and foot. This plan is inscribed: 'Mr Brown proposes for the alteration of the water at B to take away the garter, and at F to make the square toes round'.[21]

Here Brown might have been expected to suggest a cascade, but his plan does not indicate one, nor is there a tradition of one here. What does exist is a long stone tunnel some 2 feet wide and 2½ feet high which once carried the overflow unseen from an island in the old water down to the new water. Since similar tunnels once connected a small upper reservoir with the old water, and provided the outflow

19. One of the great cedars beside the lakes at Ashburnham, East Sussex.

from Brown's new water, it seems possible that Ashburnham had a personal preference for still water. True, there was once a wide cascade on the brook below Brown's lake, but this does not appear either on Brown's plan or on the estate map of 1797, and was probably made in the nineteenth century.

During his second contract Brown can hardly have found Ashburnham a cheerful place to visit. Though Jemima Ashburnham, the middle of the Earl's three daughters, had not yet been abandoned by Mr W.A. Faukner, the young man she married,[22] by 1776 Lady Ashburnham had been 'seized so suddenly with either gout or rheumatism in her head as to deprive her entirely of her senses'.[23] She was still able to visit town but remained an invalid and as a result during the Gordon Riots of 1780 had to be evacuated from Ashburnham's town house in blankets.[24] A week previously the rioting mob had torn Lord Ashburnham from his chariot.[25]

A Victorian garden now intervenes between Ashburnham House and Brown's new water, but the lakes themselves remain magnificent, delightfully backed by the hanging woods beyond. Though Brown drew two plans for bridges, the one which now crosses the stocking is of later date. Brown's greenhouse, however, survives. It

50. Brown's greenhouse at Ashburnham.

is specifically mentioned in his account book, and at £600 was a costly item for the time. Still more formidable if less elegant is a vast kitchen garden, enclosing 6 acres of land in brick walls which in places rise to 14 feet. The site is the one shown on Brown's plan and the walls may be his.

The 1760s were not only Brown's busiest period but also the years of his finest work. After Blenheim, an inspiration which stands on its own, high on the list of his great gardens — higher still among those which survive little changed — comes the Earls of Northampton's garden at Castle Ashby. His work here is also interesting because his contact with the Northamptons led to the final step in his climb from north-country garden boy to southern squire.

Brown worked for two Earls of Northampton: Charles, the Seventh, and his younger brother, Spencer, the Eighth. Charles had succeeded to his title and estates in December 1758. His mansion, part Elizabethan, part Jacobean, stood on a hilltop seven miles east of Northampton above tributaries of the River Neve, flanked by — though not so engulfingly as were some houses when Brown arrived — a phalanx of parterres which had remained unchanged since the late seventeenth century.[26] Charles was described by Lady Mary Wortley Montagu as 'lively and good natured with what is called a pretty figure. I believe he is of a humour likely to marry the first agreeable girl he gets acquainted with at London.'[27] She had perhaps met him in Venice. In the fashion of the time the Earl travelled abroad, and his taste was also fashionable. Within a year of inheriting Castle

Ashby he had asked both Brown and Robert Adam to draw plans for more fashionable gardens. The two plans survive in the Castle Ashby archives.

Though they were not dissimilar — both turned the string of small formal ponds at the bottom of the valley on the east side of the park into two largish lakes — neither was followed precisely. The final lakes are larger than either Brown or Adam proposed, Brown's grotto was never built and Adam's garden temple (the Menagerie) was built by Brown in a different place.

The year after the Seventh Earl had signed a contract with Brown (14 October 1761) he left again for the Continent, never to return. During 1763 both he and his wife died of consumption, she in Naples, he in Lyon. While he was away some of the work he had ordered was carried out. This included, in Brown's words, 'pulling down the old ice house and building a new one in a very expensive manner and place'.[28] The new ice house survives, a double-chambered cavern, the brick-lined inner chamber deep and domed. It is a monument to Brown's workmanship; though set into one end of the dam between the two lakes, it remains to this day perfectly dry.

Brown soon made contact with the new Earl, and continued with the agreed programme. He began the water works with two upper ponds, the Warren Ponds, to act as silt traps for the new lakes. And on the sloping hillside beyond he built the Menagerie-temple, probably using Adam's design. Its central dome is flanked by wings and backed by a rectangular building where the Earl kept birds rather than animals. The sale catalogue of 1774 names twenty-one species including parakeets, macaws, parrots, quails, sea pies, five sorts of pheasant, a cockatoo and a Virginia nightingale.[29] But Brown's first surviving letter to the new Earl of 8 December 1764 shows that he was soon finding him elusive:

> I fully intended myself the honour of waiting on your Lordship at Castle Ashby about ten days ago but was prevented by an information that your Lordship was not returned. I am now on my western expedition the next after it will be Northamptonshire. I shall think myself much obliged to your Lordship for an information how long your Lordship intends staying there, as also I shall think myself much obliged to Lady Northampton for an information where I can buy some of the sort of lozenges her ladyship was so obliging as to give me. If your Lordship returned to Castle Ashby I hope your Lordship found things there to your mind which is the sincere wish of my Lord
>
> Your Lordships
most obliged and most
obedient servant
Lancelot Brown.[30]

If both Earls were liable to be absentees, the Eighth had a more serious drawback. 'Lord and Lady Northampton', a contemporary letter reads, 'never paid any bills, and the rental was gone before he was aware.' 'Gaming contributed to his financial problems.'[31] After all work had ceased, in 1774, Brown had to take a charge on the timber in Yardley Chase to secure £4,080 which was still owing to him.[32] And before this, in the sixties, his landscaping was affected, as the cost of casual labour employed at Castle Ashby shows. This rose to £40 a month in 1765, fell in 1766 when the early work had been finished, rose to £52 a month in 1767 as the work on the second temple, the Dairy, and the dams for the two lakes began, peaked at £56 in 1768/1769, then fell sharply in the summer of 1769 to £30-31 a month.[33]

By this time the Earl had been involved in the greatest of all his extravagances: the notorious Northampton election campaign of 1768. By custom he and George Montagu, Fifth Earl of Halifax, had had their respective nominees elected unopposed to the town's two parliamentary seats, but now Earl Spencer of Althorp put up a rival candidate. Between them the three lords are said to have spent the colossal sum of £160,000 on bribes to electors, some of whom were paid £500 for their vote. At the poll one hundred and sixty-nine shoemakers hedged their bets and voted on both sides. Lord Spencer seemed to lose, but after an appeal to Parliament his man was declared elected, and Northampton and Halifax tossed for the other seat.[34]

It may well have been as a result of such extravagance that, when the first two lakes were finished in 1769, the third and far larger one to the north-west of the house, which Brown's plan shows and which would have formed a yet more splendid feature, was never begun.

In these years he continued to find the Earl difficult to contact. On 30 July 1766 he wrote from Trentham: 'In my way to the North I called at Ashby where I gave the best direction in my power to Mr Midgley relative to the work in general and gave some hints about the water the which he was to communicate to your Lordship on the spot and to receive such directions as your Lordship should think proper to give him and act accordingly — I wrote to Southampton to your Lordship but I presume the letter miscarried'.[35]

John Midgley was Brown's foreman at Castle Ashby (as he had been at Charlecote). Brown also called again on John Hobcroft, the carpenter and future architect in his own right, paying him for going twice to attend to the Dairy. Midgley, like Brown, seems to have needed clearer instructions. A surviving note he sent to Brown is mutilated and undated, but was probably written about this time:

Sir,

I have taken down both elms as I could not bring the ground very well together without; and I have shortened the spinny and taken down some of the limes and trim'd some up so as to let your eye through without making a avenue which when the wall is taken away will make a fine opening. I do intend not to take one of the walls down only fence high till I see his Lordship or you as you did not fix where the sunk-fence was to go.

You'l let me have twenty pounds against next Satterday night to pay the men.

From your servant
Jonathan Midgley.[36]

XX. Sandbeck, Yorkshire.

XXI. Brown's menagerie at Castle Ashby, Northamptonshire.

XXII. Beside the lake at Ashburnham, East Sussex.

XXIII. The lake at Coombe Abbey near Coventry.

Brown's letter from Trentham had continued on another subject: 'Mr Fallerton [correctly Foulerton] informed me that you and Mr Drummond had not agreed about the Huntingdon estate. If no other person is in treaty with your Lordship I shall be glad to have the refusal of it, your Lordship shall have very little trouble with me upon it I shall give an immediate answer as soon as I know the conditions and have looked it over.'[37]

This Mr Drummond was probably Henry, the Earl's banker (and brother-in-law). Brown may well have learned about the Huntingdon estate from his own banker, Robert Drummond, Henry's brother. It could also be that Henry Drummond was not a rival purchaser but was holding the estate's 'writings' as a pledge against money advanced to the Earl. There is no other obvious reason for his holding them without having bought the place.

Brown liked it. It was the Manor of Fenstanton, ten miles north-west of Cambridge. Next year on 25 May 1767, he wrote for the third time about it:

I have taken the liberty twice before this to beg to know of your Lordship whither you intend parting with the Huntingdon estate and whither I might apply to Mr Worthington [correctly Partington] for the writings the which were delivered to him by Mr Drummond. I shall be much obliged to your Lordship for an answer as I am kept in suspense and have other things on offer, but I was determined to have nothing to do with anybody 'till your Lordship had given me your answer. Your Lordship remembers that you sade I might have the estate at the price it was offered to Mr Drummond, and I promised an immediate answer after I had seen it. I am happy to hear that the gout has had so good an effect on your health....[38]

What the other places were in which Brown was interested is not known. Perhaps, like any buyer, he merely wanted to qualify his interest in the Earl's property. This did not prevent him revealing how keen he was by writing again three days later:

I have this moment received a letter from Midgley in which he informs me your Lordship desires to know when I shall be at Castle Ashby. My intention was to have been there soon after the King's birthday but he informs me your Lordship means to set out for Derbyshire on Sunday next I will defer my journey till your Lordship returns. I wrote to your Lordship last post relative to Huntingdonshire and I hope I shall be honour'd with an answer as that subject has been distressing to me. I cannot give directions about the alteration over the columns at the Dairy till I am on the spot. Your Lordship will much oblige me by mentioning the time your Lordship means to return to Ashby.[39]

Finally on 7 June he met the Earl. Next day he wrote:

I never heard one word from your Lordship relative to the estate 'till yesterday since I had the honour of waiting on your Lordship at Castle Ashby — as soon as I possibly can see it, I will, and your Lordship may depend on an immediate answer. My intentions were to have been at Castle Ashby this week, but was prevented by Midgley informing me that your Lordship was to go into Derbyshire... which determined me to go by Blenheim into Worcestershire and Staffordshire and to return to Ashby. I shall be very unhappy if your Lordship should be from home as there are many things that should be settled. I should be very happy to be informed how your Lordship's engagements stand. As soon as I can settle the number of days for my expedition I will be sure to let your Lordship know...[40]

Three months later Brown made his firm offer. By now he was home at Hampton Court.

I have received a part of the papers and survey relative to Fenstanton Estate from Mr Partington: I have been much out of order for the last five or six days which has prevented me from going into Huntingdonshire which I hope I shall be able to do very soon. My intention is to have the estate at the price your Lordship had agreed with Mr Drummond which was I think thirteen thousand pounds. It will not be very convenient for me to pay the whole of the money before Lady Day next. I could at Christmas pay six or seven thousand pounds. Your Lordship will be so good as to signify your pleasure in regard to the time of payment, and a final answer shall be sent when I have seen the estate, at which time an article may be drawn up binding both sides to the conditions that shall be thought necessary. Your Lordship will very much oblige me by an immediate answer. I hope the family are all well.[41]

Next year, 1768, Brown duly became Lord of the Manor of Fenstanton.[42]

Castle Ashby remains a splendid example of Brown's work. The little church of Grendon, perched on its hilltop, is central to the distant view. Closer comes Brown's belt of encircling trees, with typical carriageways still running through them. The Menagerie stands above its lake, looking across the valley to the Dairy beside the house. Many of the fine beeches, now nearing the ends of their lives, must be Brown's, and one huge cedar near the Menagerie can certainly be identified as his. It is this tree which Charles, the Eighth Earl's son, was told when a boy not to jump over in case he broke its top.[43]

Fenstanton, Brown's new manor, lay in flat country on the edge of the Fens, close to the Ouse; it carried with it the right to certain tolls on the river. Today it stands, not far from the church, in what has become a backwater of the main village, this in turn bypassed on the far side. The house is a small, regularly shaped one, with a tall tiled roof and a projecting porch, set surprisingly close to the road, pleasant enough in character but with little of the dignity its name suggests. Nor did Brown come here often, but retained and continued to live at Wilderness House, Hampton Court. But he was proud of his new property, so comfortingly confirming his status as a gentleman, and sent his assistant, Spyers, to make a folio of elegant maps of it, now at Cambridge University Library.

51. Brown's Dairy at Castle Ashby, Northamptonshire.

Five miles away at Hinchingbrooke lived the Fourth Earl of Sandwich, who became a friend. Sandwich is one of the few people about whom Horace Walpole is halfway polite, describing him in 1771 as 'activity, industry and knowledge in person, and the most proper man in the world to be at the head of the marine'.[44]

This was the third time Sandwich had become First Lord of the Admiralty. All his life, ships and the sea had interested him. At the age of twenty he had made a celebrated voyage round the Mediterranean, accompanied by 'a painter of considerable excellence, to draw the dresses of every country they should go into'.[45] Sandwiches were named after the Earl, however, not because he would eat them at his Admiralty desk, but because he once spent twenty-four hours at the gaming table, living on nothing but beef 'sandwiched' between slices of bread.[46]

He was a large, ungainly man — a friend once explained that he recognised him at a distance because he was 'walking down both sides of the street at once',[47] and his dancing teacher in Paris asked him to do him the favour, when he returned to London, of not revealing who had taught him to dance. He was commonly known as Jemmy Twitcher, after a character in *The Beggar's Opera*, because in the House of Lords he had betrayed his friend Wilkes by accusing him of writing *Essay on Woman*, an obscene parody of Pope's *Essay on Man*. When Sandwich tried to get himself elected as High Steward of Cambridge his supporters were called Twitcherites.[48]

At the time Brown bought Fenstanton Manor he must have known about, and perhaps even attended, the private theatricals which were the Sandwich household's evening entertainment at Hinchingbrooke. But by 1774 Sandwich had taken Miss Martha Ray, a singer, as his mistress, and 'oratorios for a week at Christmas' had been substituted. His wife, Walpole noted, 'was confined for lunacy, but Lord S.'s enemies said she was still shut up after she recovered her senses — at least she never appeared in the world again'.[49]

The affair with Miss Ray became a scandal and ballads and obscene insults were shouted from the park below Sandwich's windows; but they remained together until 1779 when a rival lover, James Hackman, once an army captain, now Vicar of Wivenhoe, lay in wait outside Covent Garden theatre, periodically refreshing himself with brandy and water, then shot Miss Ray dead as she emerged. He was hung at Tyburn, explaining that insane love had been the cause of his crime.

At the Admiralty Sandwich was able to report on, and perhaps promote, the career of Brown's second son, John, who had now joined the Navy. 'The enclosed,' he wrote to Brown on 11 April 1772, 'will show you that your son has long before this got a firm commission, as the Savage has been sailed above two months, and is of course long ago arrived at her destination. I am allways happy when it is in my power to prove the truth and regard with which I am your very sincere friend.'[50]

Sandwich also eventually helped Brown's eldest son, Lancelot, who for the time being was studying law, to obtain a seat in Parliament. Meanwhile he wrote occasionally to Brown about local political matters, and may well have proposed Brown for High Sheriff of Huntingdonshire. In 1770 Brown was appointed to this office. Though its powers were slight and duties light, the year that he held it marked the high point of his ascent of the social ladder.

Brown's private life and public duties at Fenstanton did not interrupt his professional work. He was still busy on numerous projects which he had already begun, and he continued to negotiate new commissions. One of these was for the Sixth Baron Craven at Coombe Abbey in Warwickshire.

By this time Brown could be choosy about his commissions and he might well have hesitated before undertaking to improve the grounds of Coombe Abbey. The land on which the house stood, some four miles east of Coventry, was excessively flat, and the stream which crossed the 1000 acre estate ran some way to the north. But perhaps Brown and Craven were particular friends — the only surviving intimate picture of Brown (a sketch by Cosway) shows him sitting at a table drinking with Craven — and they had already spoken about a second commission from Craven, to build a house for him and landscape the grounds at Benham in

Berkshire, a place with greater potential.

Or perhaps it was Lady Craven, born Elizabeth, daughter of the Fourth Earl of Berkeley, who wanted a great garden designed by the most fashionable gardener of the time. She was a flamboyant lady who bore Craven six children in twelve years, then became a playwright. Horace Walpole described her at the first night of her second play:

> She sat in the middle of the front row of the stage-box much dressed with a profusion of white bugles and plumes, to receive the public homage due to her sex and loveliness. It was amazing to see so young a woman entirely possess herself, but there is such integrity and frankness in her consciousness of her own beauty and talents, that she speaks of them with a naivete as if she had no property in them, but wore them as gifts from the Gods.[51]

She and Walpole were said to have had an affair, though it was her affair with the French Ambassador to England, the Duke of Guines, which ended her marriage. Suspecting this, Craven feigned a headache then followed her to a ball where he and friends broke down the door of a private room and 'found her Ladyship sitting upon the ambassador's knee, in such a state, as clearly proved that a few minutes would have brought on an amorous conflict'.[52]

Lady Craven took a patronizing view of her husband, who

> disliked reading anything but newspapers and yet he never had a dispute with his wife. He hated trouble, and constantly applied to me when he was puzzled or perplexed... His heart was naturally good... [but] his life was one continued ramble: to hunt in Leicestershire — to drive the Oxford stage-coach — to see a new play in London — to visit Lord Craven [his uncle] at Coombe Abbey, or Admiral Craven at Benham, were his continual occupations. He had a dislike to remain longer than three weeks at a time at any place: which when I had observed, he kissed my hand, and replied, 'Till I lived with you, my love, I never stayed three *days* in one place...'[53]

Of his various places (as well as Coombe Abbey and Benham, these included Hamstead Marshal, where the great house on its splendid site above the river Kennet had been burnt down, but could have been rebuilt) Craven chose Coombe Abbey to improve first. The seventeenth century gardens which Brown found here were particularly extensive. A Knyff print of 1708 shows formal parterres to east and west of the house where they stretch away three or four deep. It was easy for Brown to sweep these away but less easy to devise a replacement, since the lie of the land made it impossible to create the sort of sinuous river or lake which would span an eastern view from the house. Instead he created a lake aligned with the view. When he had finished, this view extended down a full mile of water. The contours of the land dictated that, at its far end, the tail of this 90 acre lake should double back behind a low hill. Here he erected, probably to his own design, a menagerie which included an octagonal tower with leaded dome. From the house

52. Brown's menagerie at Coombe Abbey.

the menagerie was a distant eye-catcher — though trees now put them out of sight of each other. The whole undertaking was vast, even by Brown's standards. The dam at the lake's head is half a mile in length and, at its tallest, some 20 feet high.

To the north of the lake Brown planted thickly. To the south he created an expanse of open parkland. A plan of 1778,[54] two years after the work was completed, shows that he adapted his usual technique to Coombe's flat land, planting one recognisably Brown-like clump, but otherwise only a thin scattering of trees, some in short rows, some on their own.

It was from Coombe Abbey that Brown wrote one of his few surviving letters to his wife, Bridget. He had arrived there from Fawsley in December 1775, and found the restless Lord Craven typically absent. After a day inspecting the works, he wrote from his bedroom, which was hung with pictures of various executed statesmen: Charles I, Lord Strafford, and an unknown one who 'looks as dismal as the others, on which account I conclude he was as unfortunate. I am quite alone at this place,' he continued, 'and as I had no body to talk to I have been very much upon the phylosophick strain, a day so spent it is not one of the worst we spend, and just to conclude it, I have enterd into a conversation with you which has every charm except your company which will ever be the sincere and the principal delight of, my dear Biddy, your affectionate h. Lancelot Brown.'[55]

John Byng, who visited Coombe some eleven years later, was not impressed:

Mean is the entrance to Combe Abbey, a place of which I had heard much and where my friend Capability Brown was allowed to act. So modern taste joined to antiquity I hope would produce great things, but here sadly deceived me for he has ruined old avenues and not planted in their place half enough. The water is stagnate and there is no inequality of ground... In front at a short distance is a poor attempt at a castle building, for the front of a dog kennel.[56]

The main entrance to the park survives, a far from mean but imposingly solid triumphal archway; it lies to the west of the present entrance. But the dog kennels with their crenellated front must be judged from a nineteenth century watercolour. The area to the south of the lake which Byng found underplanted, is now hidden by the dense woodland which has grown up close to the house. Between the house and the lake formal parterres were re-introduced in the nineteenth century by Nesfield, including a large knot garden, and the whole is now a playground for the citizens of Coventry, with boating ponds full of canoes and climbing frames for children among Scots pine plantations. But the view down Brown's great lake is as magnificent as ever, and the scale of his work as astonishing.

The year after Craven first wrote to Brown, in 1771, Brown made his first visit to the Duke of Ancaster at Grimsthorpe in Lincolnshire. Ancaster had been another of the fourteen to sign the petition in his support in 1758. It was at Grimsthorpe that John Grundy, the landscape engineer already mentioned for his dam-building technique, had been at work for more than twenty years.

In 1748 Grundy had proposed increasing the size of the Great Water (which already existed) by building a lower dam, but had abandoned the idea. This was limestone country, and he may have had trouble with swallow holes. Instead, he rebuilt its existing dam and raised the level of an upper water by transforming an old bridge into a dam.

So when Brown arrived, he found the landscape's main features, its two lakes, already in existence. Undaunted, he sent his assistant, Samuel Lapidge, to make surveys, and used these to produce several plans of his own. They included one for 'the boundary of the park and the fields taken into it', showing that, just as at Burghley, Alnwick and Richmond, to name only three places, the scale of Brown's projects forced his clients to turn productive agricultural land into parkland. He also produced a plan for the alteration of the ground around the house, another for 'the water in the bottom', and another for a sham bridge some 350 feet in length.[57]

In his account book he specified that this was to be placed at the head of the water which the road to Grimsthorpe went over, meaning Grundy's upper dam, but it was never built. Nor were his plans for altering the water put into effect. And since he only charged the modest sum of £105 for his plans, leaving Ancaster to decide what were fair expenses for his own and Lapidge's visits, it seems unlikely that he personally carried out any other alterations. But the Duke probably made use of his plans for the grounds around the house, and perhaps for the planting around the lakes, carrying out the work with his own labour. If the absence of Brown's splendid bridge is to be regretted, the landscape at Grimsthorpe remains today a fine one, with great lawns sweeping down from the house to the larger lake, this seeming to lie enclosed in a bowl of tree-clad hills.

53. Lord Clive of India by Nathaniel Dance.

9. Brown versus Chambers

BY 1769 Brown had been closely connected for at least four years with Sir William Chambers. Not only was this the year in which he applied to the Board of Works of which Chambers was a member, for an extension to Wilderness House, and the year in which the Board criticized his work at Hampton Court, but he had also by now worked alongside Chambers at Richmond for the King and at Blenheim for the Duke of Marlborough.[1] And in 1765 both he and Chambers had submitted plans to Lord Midleton for a house at Peper Harrow. Midleton chose Chambers's plan.

Now they were again both invited to submit plans by the same client, this time by Lord Clive of India for a new house at Claremont near Esher. Clive chose Brown's plan. Chambers, as I have suggested, probably already disapproved of Brown's style of landscaping, but this defeat in his own professional field — architecture — may have been a final provocation, and there could be some truth in the tradition that while Brown celebrated in bricks and mortar, Chambers revenged himself with pen and ink.

Claremont was important to Brown in another way. This new commission, added to all his other work, brought him to a situation often reached by successful professional men, when he had to decide whether to refuse business or take a partner. Brown solved the problem by going into partnership with Henry Holland, son of his old friend of the same name, Henry Holland the builder.

The Hollands and the Browns had not only lived fairly close to each other — the Browns at Hammersmith, the Hollands at Fulham — from the time Brown had left Stowe until he moved to Hampton Court, but Brown had worked with the older Holland for Lord Shelburne at Bowood and for the Duke of Bridgewater at Ashridge. Though the young Holland went straight into his father's firm when he was only sixteen, there is no record that he worked on either of these project.[2] By 1769, however, Brown must have recognized his talents. While Claremont intself was Brown's design, young Henry Holland was responsible for much of the internal detail.

If Brown had a good opinion of his new partner's professional abilities, equally

Holland left an important testimonial after Brown's death to his competence as an architect.

> No man that I ever met with so well understood what was necessary for all ranks and degrees of society; no one disposed his offices so well, set his buildings on such good levels, designed such good rooms, or so well provided for the approach, for the drainage, and for the comfort and convenience of every part he was concerned in. This he did without ever having had one single difference or dispute with any of his employers. He left them pleased, and they remained so as long as he lived.[3]

The old house and its grounds at Claremont had been almost as important in the development of English landscape design during the first half of the eighteenth century as Stowe had been. It was originally built for himself by the architect and playwright, Vanburgh. He had described it as his 'very small box', when he sold it to the Earl of Clare, later Duke of Newcastle, in 1714, but had agreed to enlarge it to an appropriate size for the new owner.

He also built for Newcastle a belvedere, or 'crenellated prospect-house'. Its prospects were certainly enormous. It stood on a nearby small hill and from its battlements, before the home counties disappeared under industrial haze, the dome of St Paul's could be seen in one direction and Windsor Castle in another.

Closer, the belvedere looked down on a fifty-acre pleasure garden, where Bridgeman and Kent now came to work, each transforming it according to their own styles. Between them they created a typical pleasure garden of the period, in which a succession of features — lake, grotto, temple, amphitheatre — were designed to inspire appropriate moods. The house played little part.

This stood on low ground to the south-east, and according to Clive it was damp. Certainly the site Brown chose, some distance to the north-east, was higher and therefore drier. But, far from uniting house and garden, it left them more divided. The hill with its belvedere now actually stood between them and neither could be seen from the other.

It did, however, have a fine prospect to the south-east, over a great stretch of countryside which Clive also owned. This Brown did not touch. It is interesting to wonder what he might have made of it if Clive had lived longer and commissioned him to work here. Instead Brown confined his landscaping at Claremont to comparatively small though characteristic changes in Kent's pleasure gardens.

One of these was important. He re-aligned the old Portsmouth road, so that the Mound at the opposite site of the gardens from the belvedere was included, and thus gave them a balance which they had previously lacked. He also naturalized the slopes of the amphitheatre, planting these with trees and shrubs, and extended the ha-ha.[4]

Meanwhile the building of the house itself continued until 1772. For its carcass he had baked in the grounds a million and a half white bricks — he strongly disliked red bricks, once remarking that 'a red house puts the whole valley in a

54. Claremont, Surrey. Brown's Palladian entrance.

fever'.[5] Central and most magnificent, at the top of a double flight of twenty-two steps, he set its formidable Palladian entrance. Each enormous capital cost £14, each pilaster £4 10s.[6] For the rest, the house showed a marked development from those he had designed in the 1750s — Croome Court, for example, or the new façade for Newnham Paddox. In particular, there were no square corner turrets with pointed slate roofs; these were replaced by corners with stone dressings.

55. The pale blue and white assembly hall at Claremont.

Inside, the large assembly hall, made to take a carpet 67 feet by 27 feet, which Clive had brought home from India, and to display on its walls pictures of Clive's great Indian victories, was the finest room. The pictures were never hung, and today its pale blue wall and ceiling mouldings suggest to a visitor that he is inside a Wedgwood serving dish.

Among other curious features, Brown built a tunnel and subterranean entrance to the extensive basement, so that the servants could come and go unseen. Basement and tunnel enabled him to give the house open space on all four sides, 'innocent of the litter of offices'. Its underground turning circle for wagons is now used by film-making companies for dungeon scenes.

Within the basement Brown included for Clive a great bath of grey marble, some 5 feet 6 inches deep, resembling a small swimming pool. Its purpose was medicinal. Clive had been recommended cold baths for his nervous condition.

Meanwhile, according to Macaulay, 'The peasantry of Surrey looked with myserious horror on the stately house which was rising at Claremont, and whispered that the great wicked Lord had ordered the walls to be made so thick in order to keep out the devil, who would one day carry him away bodily'.[7]

Though Clive also had a town house in Berkeley Square, and three Shropshire estates, he probably did live briefly at Claremont. When the diarist, Kilvert, went there in 1871 he was shown 'a room in the roof, low but large and comfortable', which was described as Clive's bedroom.[8] And the Claremont accounts record '3 weeks asses milk for the young ladies' — perhaps Clive's daughters, Rebecca and

Charlotte.[9] The inventory made at Claremont soon afterwards recorded that in the menagerie under the belvedere there was a zebra and foal, various breeds of deer, an African bull and seven goats, 'very troublesome', further evidence that Clive may have occupied the house. But on 22 November 1774 he died in London of an overdose of laudanum.

Brown had to wait for full settlement. By now Clive had paid him £27,612, and Clive's executors paid a further £6,000 but they argued about ways in which Brown had made variations from the contract drawings, and still owed him money as late as 1780.[10]

Forty years later one of the most significant events in British royal history took place in a room at Claremont, when George IV's daughter, Princess Charlotte, gave birth to a still-born child here, then died herself. There was national mourning on an unprecedented scale. If the child had lived, Queen Victoria would not have reigned. The house today is a Christian Science school, and remains a fine and little changed example of Brown's later work as an architect. The pleasure gardens were for a time overrun by rhododendrons and laurels but are now being conscientiously restored by the National Trust.

Well before the work was finished at Claremont, where Brown and the young Henry Holland had co-operated for the first time, Brown's older daughter, Bridget, and Holland became engaged and were married. Brown had probably expected the marriage when he took his future son-in-law into partnership. As early as 1772, one of his correspondents, a Mrs Jodrell of Manchester, knew that Bridget was engaged, and wrote to say that she was 'longing to know who the fortunate swaine is

56. The underground turning circle for wagons at Claremont.

57. The grey marble bath built at Claremont for Clive for medicinal purposes.

who will soon be blessed with your daughter's fair hand at the altar'.[11] The altar was that of St George's, Hanover Square, where Henry and Bridget were married on 11 February 1773.

Brown provided generously for the young couple. He gave Bridget a dowry and Holland £5,000 of 3 per cent consolidated stock; and he settled on them his share in the lease of Carrington Mews. Bridget and Henry at first lived off Piccadilly in Half Moon Street, where the Holland family had gone after leaving Fulham, then followed the family to Hertford Street in Mayfair, where they lived at No. 17, built by Henry the elder. During the next ten years Brown often made use of their house when in London, and it was on its doorstep that he finally collapsed and died.

Claremont was still not finished when Chambers's book appeared. It was called *Dissertation on Oriental Gardening*.[12] 'In this island,' he wrote, 'it [gardening] is abandoned to kitchen-gardeners, well skilled in the culture of salads, but little acquainted with the principles of ornamental gardening. It cannot be expected that men uneducated, and doomed by their condition to waste the rigour of life in hard labour, should ever go far in so refined, so difficult a pursuit.'[13]

This was not the first time Brown had been denigrated. Horace Walpole had originally taken a patronizing view of 'one Brown who had set up on a few ideas of Kent and Mr Southcote',[14] and continued to be critical of some of his creations, for example the mole-hill effect he had produced at Moor Park. But on the whole Brown's work had not only been demanded and paid for at high prices by the country's great landowners, but admired by experts. In 1770 Thomas Whately had written his *Observations on Modern Gardening*, which had included, as well as a comment on the 'multiplicity' of Stowe's garden buildings, the approving descriptions of Wotton and Blenheim already quoted.

Chambers's attack must therefore have shocked Brown. 'Peasants emerge from the melon ground,' Chambers wrote clearly referring to Brown, 'to take the periwig and turn professor.'[15] Secure as Brown now must have seemed to outsiders, by a long way the most wanted man in his profession, lord of a manor, recently High Sheriff of his county, he must have remained sensitive about his humble family background.

Attacks of this sort showed the straightforward jealousy of a trained professional for an untrained genius. And some of Chambers's other comments were so transparently inaccurate that they should not have hurt. 'Whole woods have been swept away,' he wrote, 'to make room for a little grass and a few American weeds. Our virtuosi have scarcely left an acre of shade, not three trees growing in a line, from Land's End to the Tweed, and if their humour for devastation continues to rage much longer there will not be a forest-tree left standing in the whole Kingdom.'[16] After lakes, trees in their thousands were the most prominent feature of Brown's landscapes. Other proposals of Chambers, however, attacked the underlying aims of everything that Brown had spent the last twenty years creating.

As Chambers's title suggested, his theories (and indeed his own work at Kew) were based on a genuine admiration for Chinese gardens, acquired during visits he had made to China as a young merchant. But below these lay the far more fundamental proposal for a return to the creation of gardens in which nature was supplemented by art.

> Nature affords us but few materials to work with. Plants, ground and water, are her only productions: and though both the forms and arrangements of these may be varied to an incredible degree, yet have they but few striking varieties, the rest being of the nature of changes rung upon bells...
>
> Art must therefore supply the scantiness of nature; and not only be employed to produce variety, but also novelty and effect: for the simple arrangements of nature are... too familiar to excite any strong sensations in the mind of the beholder, or to produce any uncommon degree of pleasure.[17]

The Chinese, Chambers continued, aimed to create scenes of three different sorts: 'the pleasing, the terrible, and the surprizing'. In reverse order, the surprising, or supernatural scenes, hurried the passenger 'by steep descending paths to subterraneous vaults, divided into apartments, where lamps, which yield a faint glimmering light, discover the pale images of ancient kings and heroes, reclining on beds of state; their heads are crowned with garlands of stars, and in their hands are tablets of moral sentences: flutes, and soft harmonious organs, impelled by subterraneous waters, interrupt, at stated intervals, the silence of the place, and fill the air with solemn melody'.

The scenes of terror were 'composed of gloomy woods, deep vallies inaccessible to the sun, impending barren rocks, dark caverns, and impetuous cataracts rushing down the mountains from all parts... Bats, owls, vultures, and every bird of prey flutter in the groves; wolves, tigers and jackalls howl in the forests; half-famished animals wander upon the plains; gibbets, crosses, wheels, and the whole apparatus of torture, are seen from the roads; and in the most dismal recesses of the woods... are temples dedicated to the king of vengeance, deep caverns in the rocks, and descents to subterraneous habitations, overgrown with brushwood and brambles.'[18] In short, in exaggerated form, Chambers was asking for the ruins and grottos of thirty years before, supplemented by free-range menageries.

The pleasing scenes were 'composed of the gayest and most perfect productions of the vegetable world; intermixed with rivers, lakes, cascades, fountains, and water-works of all sorts.' While round the house were scenes, also 'chiefly of the pleasing kind', in which 'the grounds are laid out with great regularity, and kept with great care: no plants are admitted that intercept the view of the buildings; ...for they hold it absurd to surround an elegant fabric with disorderly rude vegetation; saying, that it looks like a diamond set in lead'.[19] The formal avenues, water works and parterres of the late seventeenth and early eighteenth centuries fitted such a description far more closely than anything Brown ever created.

Chambers's book had been keenly awaited. On 9 May 1772 Horace Walpole wrote to William Mason: 'The newspapers tell me that Mr Chambers the architect, who has Sir-Williamized himself, by the desire as he says of the Knights of the Polar Star, his brethren... is going to publish a treatise on ornamental gardening; that is, I suppose, considering a garden as subject to be built upon...'[20]

But when the *Dissertation* appeared, Chambers turned out to have undermined his serious suggestions not only by the exaggerated form in which he expressed them, but by his transparent and vicious attacks on Brown. A fortnight later, after Walpole had read a copy, he wrote again to Mason. 'It is more extravagant than the worst Chinese paper, and is written in wild revenge against Brown: the only surprising consequence is, that it is laughed at, and it is not likely to be adopted, as I expected; for nothing is so tempting to fools, as advice to deprave taste.'[21]

Not everybody took Brown's side. In April 1773 Oliver Goldsmith wrote to Chambers; 'Most of the companies that I now go into divide themselves into two parties, the Chamberists and the Brownists, but depend upon it you'll in the end have victory because you have Truth and Nature on your side. Mr Burke was advising me about four days ago to draw my pen in defence of your System, and sincerely I am most warmed in the Cause'.[22]

And in 1773 Joseph Cradock introduced into his *Village Memoirs* a caricature version of Brown named Mr Lay-out, 'designer in taste and gardens'.

Mr Lay-out thinks there should be a clump, and there is one: the squire thinks it would look pretty to cut a vista through it, and it is cut; and his sister thinks she should like a dairy house near the spot, and she builds it... By what I see of the intended alterations of the water, it is destined to take any course but its own; for

58. Sir William Chambers by Sir
    Joshua Reynolds.

the merit of every thing seems to consist only in the sum it is to cost: where the
genius of the place is attended to I am as much delighted as any man with
modern improvements; but where expense is only considered, or mistaken as
another name for real taste, I feel so much disgust, that I turn away my eyes
from false ornament to contemplate nature herself in a simple form, unbroken in
upon by a Mr Lay-out.[23]

The same year, however, William Mason, perhaps assisted by Walpole, made
the most celebrated contribution to the controversy when he published his *An
Heroic Epistle to Sir William Chambers*. In it he sardonically called on Art to come to
Richmond where

> untutor'd Brown
> Destroys those wonders which were once thy own.
> Lo, from his melon-ground the peasant slave
> Has rudely rush'd, and levell'd Merlin's Cave;
> Knock'd down the waxen Wizzard, seiz'd his wand,
> Transform'd to lawn what late was Fairy land;
> And marr'd, with impious hand, each sweet design
> Of Stephen Duck, and good Queen Caroline.[24]

Stephen Duck was the rustic poet already mentioned who was patronized by George II's Queen Caroline, one-time keeper of Merlin's cave, and who subsequently committed suicide in a trout stream behind the Black Lion at Reading. This was not all, Mason continued, for —

> Monkies shall climb our trees, and lizards crawl;
> Huge dogs of Tibet bark in yonder grove,
> Here parrots prate, there cats make cruel love;
> In some fair island will we turn to grass
> (With the Queen's leave) her elephant and ass.
> Giants from Africa shall guard the glades,
> Where hiss our snakes, where sport our Tartar maids...[25]

In four years Mason's poem went into fourteen editions, so it is hardly surprising that Brown is said to have had a copy.[26] But as ever he published no reply. Though his letters show that he was well able to express himself in writing when necessary, his principal interest was in his art itself, not in the construction of theories to justify it.

He seems, nevertheless, to have protested in private. Chambers, disturbed at the hostile reception of his *Dissertation*, soon published a second edition — together with *An Explanatory Discourse* under the pseudonym of Tan Chetqua, a Chinese sculptor. He now claimed that he had been attacking the whole fraternity of modern English gardeners, not just 'yon stately gentleman in the black perriwig, as he has been pleased to maintain'.[27] Brown was presumably well known for his black wig, though his portrait by Nathaniel Dance shows him wearing a fair one.

It is curious that William Mason and Oliver Goldsmith, supporters of Brown and Chambers respectively, should both have taken sides for reasons which had little to do with the aesthetics of gardening. Mason, a gardener himself, whose best remembered creation is the flower garden at Nuneham Courtenay, genuinely admired Brown's landscapes, but also believed, along with Chambers, that gardens should have 'picturesque variety', and in particular the colour and fragrance of flowers. In his long poem, 'The English Garden', he wrote:

> Well I know
> That in the general landscape's broad expanse
> Their little blooms are lost — but here are glades
> Where, if enamell'd with their rainbow hues,
> The eye would catch their splendour.[28]

What Mason disliked was Chambers's proposed use of foreign ideas for the improvement of an art which should essentially be English. He was a Whig of the old 'Patriot' school, and agreed with Walpole that 'The English taste in gardening is... the growth of the English constitution and must perish with it'.[29]

Goldsmith, on the other hand, disliked Brown's landscaping because of its social consequences: the sweeping away of villages and their arable fields to make ornamental parks. His poem, 'The Deserted Village', probably also written about Nuneham Courtenay, reveals his feelings about such antisocial landscaping.

> Thus fares the land by luxury betrayed...
> The mournful peasant leads his humble band
> And while he sinks, without one arm to save,
> The country blooms, a garden and a grave.[30]

Walpole's contribution to the controversy was confined at the time to comments in his letters and the help he probably gave Mason with the *Heroic Epistle*. He had already written his *History of Modern Taste in Gardening*, but this was not published till ten years later (1780). As the title suggests, it offered an orderly history of the gardening developments which had led to the general acceptance of Brown's 'natural' style.

In the year following the first publication of the *Dissertation* Brown again found himself working at the same place as Chambers: Milton Abbey in Dorset. The abbey was the property of Joseph Damer, who in due course became Baron Milton. Horace Walpole described him as 'the most arogant and proud of men, with no foundation but great wealth and a match with the Duke of Dorset's daughter. His birth and parts were equally mean and contemptible'.[31] Walpole estimated his income at £23,000 a year, largely inherited from an Irish great-uncle, and this was supplemented in 1768 by a further £7,000 a year from an uncle.[32]

Milton's house consisted of the remains of the old abbey. Close behind it stood the magnificent Abbey Church, and beside this (though it is hard to believe today) a flourishing small town of five or six hundred people, with four inns, a well known brewery, shops, almshouses and a grammar school.

Though Lord Milton soon had some alterations made to the house (by John Vardy, William Kent's principal successor), for the most part he turned his back on church and town, and began to improve his grounds to the north and east of the abbey. Here they fell to a valley, then rose to shapely hills, ideal conditions for a Brown landscape, and in 1763 Milton called for Brown; he began to pay him that year and signed a contract with him the next. Brown's connections with Milton Abbey thus went back much further than Chambers's, though Milton was already employing Chambers to build him a London house in Park Lane, on the site later occupied by the Dorchester Hotel.

For the next six or seven years Brown landscaped at Milton, smoothing the near side of the valley which he sowed with 1,120 lbs of Dutch clover[33] and planting trees on the far side. His account book shows payments from Lord Milton of £2,052 8s during these years. It was part of Brown's plan to create a lake in the valley, which seemed, and still seems, to invite one, but none was at this time attempted.

Milton now turned his attention to the house, and accepted a plan from Chambers to Gothicize it. The progress of this work and the steady deterioration of his relationship with Chambers went hand in hand. They quarrelled mainly about money. 'In the annual money debate between Lord Milton and me,' Chambers wrote to another client, Lord Pembroke, 'for he never parts with a guinea without a dispute...'[34] Chambers's travelling expenses soon became the central issue, Milton claiming that the commission to rebuild the abbey was large enough for him to waive them, Chambers saying that he would let down his fellow architects if he did so and getting James Paine to support him with details of the conditions of his own contracts for Wardour Castle and Thorndon Hall.

Milton then — if Chambers can be believed — began to spread rumours about Chambers's dishonesty, including the suggestion that he had cheated Lord Pembroke out of £250 for a lead roof. 'Unfortunately for me,' Chambers wrote to Pembroke, 'I have these three or four years past been building a cursed Gothick house for this unmannerly imperious Lord, who has treated me as he does everybody, ill,' and asking for 'a few lines to show the world and prove to the mighty Lord, that I am not the thief his malice represents me...' for '... it is vain to reason with Lord Milton who knows no reason but his interest; and as vain to expect fair treatment from him, who uses everybody brutally.'[35] Finally in March 1774, when much of the building had been begun but foundations for a large part of the west range still not laid, he wrote to Milton:

> The laying the new foundations must necessarily be done by me, else I should leave you in a labyrinth which probably neither your Lordship, nor your Lordship's new architect, would know how to get out of... I have now compleated three fourths of your great work, and though you have used me hardly, I will certainly go through with the rest; at least as far as relates to the carcass... I must however acquaint your Lordship that I can serve you no longer than till Christmas next, when the whole outside of your building will be compleately finished, and any other man may do the remainder without difficulty.[36]

Chambers left — James Wyatt finished the house — but before he went he supplied an outline scheme for carrying out the final part of Milton's plan to create for himself a great country seat, set apart from the vulgar classes. This was the complete removal, from its place at his back door, of the town of Milton, and the rehousing of its people in a new village a mile away.

At the same time Brown had begun to visit Milton Abbey again. He came at least twice in 1773 and again in 1774, 1775 and 1776, and received four further payments of £105 each from Milton, one of which, as he noted in his account book, was for plans for the new village. Since Milton and Chambers now parted it seems probable that Brown's plan, not Chambers's was used, and that he returned periodically to supervise its execution.

This was by no means the end of the story. Though some of the villagers agreed to be bought out, others did not. As late as 1780 a solicitor named Harrison, who had two houses and four plots at Milton was still refusing to move, so Milton had the dam of the Abbot's old fish pond opened and Harrison's house flooded. And still later, in 1784 and 1785, he was forced to promote bills in Parliament to have

59. White-rendered, thatched cottages line the street in Milton Abbas, Dorset.

the Grammar School moved. The first failed, the second succeeded.[37]

Meanwhile the new village was being built, including a church from the stones of the old tithe barn, and almshouses, which seem to have been taken down and re-erected in precisely their original form except that Milton substituted his own arms for those of the founder, John Tregonwell. Church and almshouses stood on opposite sides of the new street which, below and above, was lined with identical pairs of white-rendered thatched cottages. Behind these on both sides the combe rose steeply and is now thickly wooded.

Brown's creation of this new village is yet more proof of his versatility. His apparently friendly relations with a difficult man like Milton over about fifteen years are further evidence of his tact and ability to please his clients. But not all contemporaries admired Milton Abbas. To some it seemed inappropriate that the poor should occupy these small replicas of the mansions of the rich. 'A very miserable mistake in his Lordship,' Fanny Burney wrote in 1791, 'for the sight of common people and of the poor labouring or strolling in and about these dwellings, made them appear rather to be reduced from better days than flourish in a primitive or natural state.'[38]

Modern occupants have the opposite complaint, finding the cottages damp and sunless. As a result the horse chestnuts, which once stood picturesquely between each pair and were perhaps Brown's, but which produced much shade and dripped onto the thatch, have been removed. To the outsider Milton Abbas remains one of the most snugly picturesque villages in the country.

60. William Pitt the Elder, 1st Earl of Chatham; painted in about 1754 at the studio of W. Hoare.

10. Brown for Pitt

 IN THE SAME YEAR that Chambers published his *Dissertation* and in the following year (1773) Brown became involved with two gardens where the parts he played have till recently seemed curiously similar. One was at Harewood House in Yorkshire, the other at Wardour Castle in Wiltshire.

At both there had been an earlier contact about which little is known. At both there followed a long period during which others were making major landscape changes. At both, one of these others was Richard Woods, the Essex surveyor and gardener already mentioned for his work at Belhus. At both Brown was now called back, and his responsibility for the final result has for years been assumed. At both, however, this responsibility is now questioned.

Brown first came to Harewood in 1758. In this year the Harewood steward, Samuel Popplewell, wrote to the gardener at Castle Howard, mentioning Brown's visit.[1] Brown may even have submitted plans,[2] but Popplewell in his cash book only records a payment of £21 to Brown so this seems unlikely. Popplewell's correspondence with Edwin Lascelles, owner of Harewood, is the basis of almost everything we know about the following years there, and it suggests that for about fourteen of these Brown did not reappear.

Lascelles had inherited his estate (and a handsome fortune of £166,666 made by his father in the West Indian sugar trade)[3] in 1753, but it was parliamentary affairs rather than business which kept him in London and so produced this correspondence. His old house, Gawthorpe, stood low down in a valley, below one edge of the future lake; when the lake is low its foundations can still be seen. In 1759 the splendid new house, to be called Harewood, was begun, on the same side of the valley but high up above the old one. Long before this, however, Lascelles had been instructing Popplewell about tree planting. 'Take advantage of this open and rainy weather,' he wrote in November 1755, 'and plant and rail about as fast as possible.'[4] He ordered beds to be prepared for trees, and sent two hundred 'Newfoundland Eastern Spruce firs' in an attempt to introduce species which 'will be more likely to succeed in that barren soil'.[5]

As the house grew he continued to give instructions about trees, his letters

61. Edwin Lascelles, Lord Harewood (1712-1795) by George Knapton.

making it clear that he was concerned not only with them as potential wood and timber, but as features in the house's landscape. 'I think the beauty of a country consists chiefly in the wood,' he wrote, 'and therefore I had rather not have one tree cut to the east of the house as they stand thick in the hedgerow and will from the dining room of the new house have the appearance of a large wood.'[6]

He also ordered the removal of a large hill which once stood behind the old house and would have interrupted the descending sweep of land below the new one. This vast project took between ten and forty-five men ten years.

It was in these years that Richard Woods was at Harewood. In 1764 Lascelles paid him £56 14s for 'setting out the grounds'. His work seems to have been completed by 1766 when another gardener, Thomas White, was paid precisely the same amount.[7]

Whatever they did, Lascelles ultimately turned to Brown who returned to Harewood in 1772. He then supplied a 'plan for the intended water'.[8] This was the large lake at the valley bottom which became the central feature of the landscape, unifying all that had been done before.

62. The lake at Harewood, Yorkshire.

By 1774 Brown was moving earth, for on 23 May Popplewell wrote: 'I think Mr Brown will soon be weary of his 3 wheeld carts in that flat ground, for I am convinced that one horse will draw half as much more in a light 2 wheeld one'.[9] But it was not till 17 May 1775, that Popplewell was able to write, 'I am glad that you have got a plan from Mr Brown'.[10]

Two years later the lake was ready for filling. The results of the first attempt were disastrous. 'The beginning of last week,' Popplewell wrote to Lascelles,

we sent down the plug at the damhead, and you will if possible be more surprised than I was when I tell you that the water ran out half as fast as it came in. Upon the strictest examination we found no remedy but opening the head to the bottom where the trunk lyed; Sanderson set on as many hands as could work. Where we came to the bottom we found that the water has made it's way through the clay wall close by the south side of the trunk:– however we have now

63. View across Brown's landscape, looking from the south-east towards Harewood House.

secured it and upon putting down the plug yesterday we find it stops effectually, and we shall tomorrow compleat the whole.[11]

Lascelles had other reasons for being dissatisfied. In March next year he told Popplewell:

Mr Brown was with me the other day to desire I would give him a draft for the remaining £400, part of the £900 which he was not to desire until the whole was certified and allowed to be done according to contract. I have always said and did insist upon it that the ground was scandalous lay'd, and beggarly sown, and that several other parts were slovenly run over and badly finished, particularly by the island. Mr Brown assures me that he will be at Harewood House, on purpose to meet me and give me satisfaction before Easter.[12]

How right was Lascelles? There is plenty of evidence to show that he was cautious with his money and allowed his servants no extravagances. He said as much himself, writing to Popplewell, 'if I am conscious of a great expense, and what done for it doth not appear adequate, who hath a better right to find fault than myself?'[13] In Yorkshire style, he liked to get value for money and to pay for work, not promises. There is equally little doubt about Brown's response. When he was criticized (his difference with Griffin at Audley End was a rare exception) he regularly promised to put right what was wrong. And Lascelles, in spite of his indignation, paid Brown his £400, and within the year, another £400.[14]

Today Harewood remains a magnificent landscape. In Brown's time, as contemporary illustrations show, the drop below the house was more immediate (there is now a terrace, built by Sir Charles Barry in the 1840s) but the effect is still to magnify the lakeside meadow, creating a strange uncertainty about the size of the black St Kilda sheep which graze there. Beyond the lake the hills rise steeply, part bare, part wooded, to a thickly planted skyline. The effect is of a deep bosky bowl, on a grand scale. Though new research has shown that Lascelles, Woods, White and even Popplewell all played their parts here, Brown, who came last, must be given most of the credit.

I doubt whether the same can be said about Wardour Castle. When the Eighth Lord Arundell had inherited this in 1756 its only important building was Old Wardour Castle, a ruin since an ancestor had pulled it down during the Civil War. Lord Arundell was only sixteen. For some years he was abroad on the Grand Tour, and anyway did not have the money to build or landscape, but after he had married the wealthy Mary Conquest, only daughter of Benedict Conquest, he began to consider improvements.

At first he thought of rebuilding the old castle. Joseph Spence, in his unpublished 'Hints for Wardour', 29 July 1763, made suggestions for changes to the surrounding grounds, and these include three references to 'Mr Brown's plan'.[15] Of all the new evidence about Wardour, this is the least easy to fit into a coherent sequence of events. Such a plan by Brown has never been found, and is mentioned by no one else. The opening sentence of Lord Arundell's letter to Brown of 1773 (see below) makes it even more surprising that Brown should already have provided a plan ten years earlier. Possibly Arundell's memory was short, or he never knew of this earlier plan by Brown, but neither of these are persuasive suggestions.

Whatever the truth, by the following year (1764) Richard Woods was working at Wardour. In this year he made a full plan for the grounds,[16] to which he later added the new castle, though this was not begun till 1770. It was to stand a mile from the old castle, high up above the broad valley of the little river Sem. The position was a fine one. The old castle became a feature at the left-hand extremity of the new castle's view, while the Sem crossed from here till it passed out of sight to the right.

Woods's plan showed a swan-shaped lake near the old castle, a second elongated lake close below it, then a series of small ponds crossing below the new castle but some way closer to it than the Sem. Along the course of the Sem he showed what seem to be three natural lakes. The Sem and his new string of ponds were to meet to the south-west of the new castle, where there was to be a far more dramatic lake, filling this entire end of the valley.

During the next six or seven years the Arundell archives show conclusively that Woods created the Swan Lake, possibly by expanding a previous pond, and started work on the second lake close below it. But neither his string of small canals and ponds, nor the big lake were made. During this time Woods also created a number of garden features which have been previously credited to Brown. He planted the Lady Grove to the east of the house, built within it an ice house and a Gothic temple, built the kitchen garden with its orangery, and created a ha-ha.[17]

By 1771 Arundell seems to have lost patience with Woods. Perhaps the new castle (designed by James Paine) was costing more than he expected and he was trying to economize. In this year Woods wrote him a pathetic letter, denying that he was expensive.

> What makes it so, my Lord, is the multiplicity of business I've always had to settle each time, which generally keeps me 9 or 10 days or sometimes more. Your Lordship thinks a guinea a day, which would not be sufficient to keep myself, horses and servant, considering how many broken days in a year I have, for example take out Sundays, many days ill by getting colds etc. how many days and nights in town at expences, merely to wait on gentlemen without even charging anything for it, how many days in a year are spent at home only in answering letters, and add to that the great expense in a year for postage let all these disadvantages be balanc'd against all the days I could make at a guinea a day, and I believe it would be easily prov'd that I should soon be oblig'd to give over traveling, unless like a Tom Tinker. If the gentleman your Lordship is pleased to mention had done business upon those terms, I know not how he could have raised a fortune at £2,500 per annum...[18]

'The gentleman' was almost certainly Brown.

Arundell did not relent, and in August 1773 wrote the letter to Brown already mentioned:

> ... as I am making improvements here, I have long thought of desiring you to come here, and having seen several specimens of your fine taste, I am come to a resolution of having a general plan from you for the grounds, water etc., and as I am inform'd you are to be some time this summer in my neighbourhood, I should be glad you would fix a time please and let me know beforehand that I may not be from home... I hope it may be convenient for you to spend some days with me to take a full view of this place which I flatter myself will be worthy your attention...![19]

Brown was ill and did not come. In December Arundell wrote again:

64. A nineteenth-century view of the banqueting hall across the Swan Lake at Wardour, Wiltshire. The ruins of the old castle are in the background.

I am very sorry to hear of your indisposition and that it prevented me the pleasure of seeing you here, which I have long wished for, being convinc'd it is needless to go on with anything in the grounds till you have taken a view of it, and I flatter myself you will find room to show your fine taste. I intend going to town for the winter about the latter end of January, and should be very happy if it would suit you to make me a visit here about the 20th or before...[20]

Brown must in due course have arrived because in 1775 he produced his plan.[21] Its two main features, the Swan Lake and the great lake to the south-west of the new castle are very similar to those of Woods's plan. Perhaps Arundell had shown him Woods's plan, but there is no need to accuse him of copying it. The Swan Lake had already been made, and the contours of the valley to the south-west would have given any lake in this area much the same shape. Furthermore, Brown eliminated Woods's string of minor ponds and canals, giving his plan an elegance which Woods's lacks. Once again, however, the great lake was not made. What survives at Wardour, and indeed already existed by the time Brown drew his plan, were the three smaller lakes on the course of the Sem, which Woods's plan had also shown, and two more, also on the Sem, which would have been engulfed on both plans by the great new lake. All five are shown on the Andrews and Dury map of Wiltshire published two years earlier.

Here, they appear naturally shaped, but as they survive today, much neglected, each is supported by a dam. It is with these lakes that Brown has been credited, and perhaps he did build their dams. But there are two reasons for suggesting that he did not. These dams would have involved far more work than damming the Sem lower down, to create the one great lake. And for the work on these five dams there would surely have been a contract, visits by Brown, more letters and more payments. As it is, nothing has been found except a single payment of £84 in 1780 — an appropriate amount for a visit and a plan.[22]

Of the remaining garden features which have sometimes been claimed as Brown's, the banqueting hall built in the curtain wall of the old castle is also clearly shown on the Andrews and Dury map of 1773, so predates his plan. The grotto, in the same area, was built later by a local Tisbury mason, Josiah Lane.[23] Only the Dairy Temple near the new castle might be his.

When nothing certain can be said about Brown's work at a particular place, he is often credited with the tree planting. In *Excursions from Bath*, 1801, however, the author writes of Wardour, 'The ground is broken by plantations, suggested by Mr Wood of Essex, the judiciousness of which Brown himself had the taste to admire, and fortitude to applaud evincing his sincerity by frequent visits to the spot.'

It seems, in conclusion, that Brown did as little at Wardour as he did much at Harewood. The new evidence about both places also suggests that the descendants of great eighteenth century landowners often exaggerated Brown's contributions to their landscapes and forgot those of less well-known designers.

Now that Brown owned a property only ten miles from Cambridge he had friends at the university. It was probably one of these, John Mainwaring, Professor of Theology at St John's, who persuaded him to redesign part of the gardens of this college.

Mainwaring was a keen gardener himself (and a friend of William Mason's). He spent his vacations at his small property of Caer Caradoc near Church Stretton on the Welsh borders, where he had married the parson's sister and later held the living himself. While she was buxom and extrovert, he was a hypochondriac, so much so that 'the whole university of Cambridge equally expressed their surprise at this wonderful contrast'. He spent his time 'looking every hour at the thermometer, and sending for his clogs, lest a stone floor should strike chill to his feet', and would stop up 'every creek or window' with cork.[24]

At Church Stretton Mainwaring had landscaped his own small garden, which he was keen to show Brown. But if it was he who first suggested Brown to St John's, it was Dr Powell, Master of the College, who persuaded its fellows to accept Brown's estimate of £800, by suggesting an appeal to old members and contributing £500 himself.[25] That was in February 1773 by which time the college had already used Brown to repair the bank of the Cam where this passed through its gardens. His new, £800 scheme was for the Fellows' Garden. This he transformed from an old bowling green and small formal area known as the Walks into a wilderness. The

Wilderness became its name.

An eighteenth century wilderness, far from being what it suggests, was a garden feature as carefully defined and specifically planted as any seventeenth century parterre, even if the aim — naturalness — was entirely different. Philip Miller, in his gardening dictionary of 1768 describes exactly how one should be made and what plants it should include, distinguishing carefully between parts where deciduous and evergreen trees would predominate.

In the deciduous parts beside the walks should come 'primroses, violets, daffodils, and many other sorts of wood flowers, not in a straight line but rather to appear accidental, as in a natural wood'. Behind these there should be shrubs of increasing sizes, rising to laburnums and lilacs then finally to standard deciduous trees. In the evergreen parts the walks should first be lined with 'laurustinus, boxes, spurge laurel, juniper, savin and other dwarf evergreens', then should come evergreen shrubs of increasing sizes, rising to yews, cypresses and finally firs and pines. 'The manner of separating the evergreens from the deciduous trees', Miller continued, 'will not only make a better appearance, but also cause them to thrive far beyond what they usually do when intermixed.' This, however, was advice which Brown in his clumps sometimes ignored, for example at Tottenham Park where he specifically recommended mixing evergreens with broadleaf trees.

65. The Backs, Cambridge, looking towards St. John's College.

The only work a wilderness required, Miller concluded, was 'to mow and roll the large grass walks, and to keep the other ground free from weeds'. And to prune the trees by cutting out dead or irregular branches. 'This being the whole labour of a Wilderness, it is no wonder they are so generally esteemed, especially when we consider the pleasure they afford.'[26]

The fellows of St John's seem to have recognized that there would be no profit for Brown from his £800 scheme, and in gratitude gave him a piece of silver plate costing £50, for his transformation of their garden. One wild corner of this — the Dell — today suggests what he achieved. The rest suffered even more severely than most gardens from Dutch Elm disease — about five hundred were lost — but compensates with a colourful display of spring bulbs.

Professor Mainwaring's Shropshire garden was one of those Brown meant to visit in 1773. His travels this year give a good idea of the sort of active professional life which, at the age of fifty-six, he was still leading. In February he went to the west country via Reading and Tottenham Park. This was the visit for which Lord Bruce organized such elaborate preparations, ordering the gate to be left open for him and a bed aired. The journey included a call at Milton Abbas to supervise the early work on Lord Milton's new village. In June he was almost certainly at Benham in Berkshire, to consult Lord Craven about the house and grounds there, and probably at Milton Abbas again. In August he went to the west to visit one of Clive's Shropshire properties, Oakley Park. Perhaps Clive was thinking of commissioning him here as well as at Claremont. It was on this trip that he had hoped to visit Professor Mainwaring at Caer Caradoc, but did not have time.[27]

If, in earlier years, Brown had probably ridden or travelled by stage coach he now went in his own carriage. In the early 1770s he had described to his daughter his fast drive to Broadlands, Hampshire, when he successfully proved his son, John, wrong about how quickly it would be possible to drive to Plymouth. Two years later (1775), in the west again, he reported that 'the post boys were so obliging as to take me through a river that filled my chaise with water'.[28] In his will he left to his wife his chariot or coach, two coach horses and a saddle horse.

By September he was touring his northern commissions, including Brocklesbury, Burton Constable, Harewood, Scampston and possibly Temple Newsam. This, in addition, was the year in which his daughter Bridget married. It is scarcely surprising that although Arundell had written to him in August, work then illness prevented him from reaching Wardour till the following year.

For one of these northern clients, Sir William St Quintin of Scampston, Brown did not undertake the landscaping himself but merely provided plans. Quintin's father, also Sir William, who had made Scampston famous for its thoroughbred stud, had previously had a plan drawn up, probably by Charles Bridgeman, [29]for a formal garden with a large T-shaped pond, but this may never had been made. His son inherited the property in 1770 and soon consulted Brown, who, when he came to Scampston, which lies in the Vale of Pickering between the Yorkshire Moors and

XXIV. Claremont, Surrey.

XXV. Distant view of Milton Abbas, Dorset, showing how picturesquely the village is tucked into its setting.

XXVIII. Brown almost certainly designed the crenellated Gothic deer house at Scampston, Yorkshire.

Wolds, found one of the flattest estates he was ever called to improve, on a par with Lord Dacre's land at Belhus. But at least a beck flowed through the grounds of Scampston.

Brown's plan dammed the Scampston Beck in two places, creating a long crescent-shaped pair of lakes, which encircled the inner park. Between them he put a cascade, and at the lower dam another. Here he built a small Palladian bridge with a blank back wall, modelled perhaps on the similar but much larger one at Stowe.

St Quintin was pleased; writing to thank Brown for the cascade plan, he gave details of the work as it was progressing, some parts of which were his own additions:'... I have made the sunk fence on both sides of the gateway, which has a most charming effect. I have also fill'd the angle of the water at the west end, and have also made an island where the water was too broad, and have widen'd it to the north of the bridge according to your plan, which answers prodigiously well, for which I return you many thanks. I shall be in London some time next month, and will certainly wait on you. I beg your acceptance of some Yorkshire hams... '[30] Scampston was still known in this century for the excellence of its hams.

Forty years later John Bigland wrote that 'the judicious taste' of Sir William St Quintin had 'greatly improved the scenery' and 'a sterile plain destitute of every natural advantage has, at a considerable expense, been rendered beautiful by art'.[31]

Today the lake, the Palladian bridge and the island survive. So do fine clumps of trees in the park, both within and beyond the lakes, but the cascade between the lakes failed some years ago and was rebuilt in concrete.

Further from the house, however, in the old deer park, lies the estate's only hill — hillock might be a better word — today set about with ancient well spaced Scots pines. For this Brown almost certainly designed the delightful crenellated Gothic deer house, so described because its rear part gave the deer shelter in winter. Its decorative trefoil and its Gothic windows suggest those of Brown's orangery at Burghley. In his time it would have been stuccoed, but its exposed rose-coloured bricks, baked on the estate, today add to its charm.

During the 1770s, Brown was concerned for different reasons about each of his two older sons. Lancelot, the elder, after leaving Eton had studied law at Lincoln's Inn, and by 1773 was a qualified barrister. At least one of Brown's clients, William Constable of Burton Constable (who in the 1750s had rejected the splendidly ornate ceiling design which Brown then used at Corsham) was promising young Lancelot work. 'Whenever I deal in law,' Constable wrote to Brown, 'which, by the way, I have often been subject to, the young chancellor shall be troubled with my grievances. A graft from genius cannot fail where so many blocks allmost flourish.'[32]

By the following year, however, Lancelot was trying to make use of his father's connections in another way — to get himself a seat in Parliament. He went to Sir

66. View from Brown's Palladian bridge at Scampston, Yorkshire.

James Lowther of Lowther Hall in Westmorland. Outside Northumberland, Lowther Hall had been one of Brown's earliest commissions in the north, and he had produced a particularly elegant plan[33] for major improvements which were successfully carried out.

Lowther was a man of enormous wealth. When he came of age in 1757 he was reckoned the richest commoner in England. The following year he had been another of the young men seen by Horace Walpole paying absurd prices at Schaub's painting auction (see page 127). Three years later when he married, Walpole wrote: 'The great prince of the coalpits, Sir James Lowther, marries the eldest infanta of the adjoining coal pits, Lord Bute's daughter'.[34]

Such wealth 'acquired at an age when his mind was still unformed and easily perverted... appeared to disturb his mental balance.'[35] His mania took the form of a ruthless determination to control all five of his local parliamentary constituencies, not to mention the boroughs of Lancaster, Wigan and Durham in the north, and of Haslemere in Surrey.[36] From these he could normally count on getting nine of his own candidates elected; in Parliament they were known as his 'Ninepins'. He ruthlessly pressurized the voters in his constituencies. When those of Whitehaven displeased him he threatened to ruin the town by closing its mines and iron works, sacking its seamen and cancelling its farmers' leases. In another borough, with the collusion of the mayor, he had an extra 1447 freemen created to vote for him. 'These, from the rapidity of their growth, were wittily termed "Mushrooms", and Sir James... was nicknamed Jimmy Graspall, Earl of Toadstall.'[37]

He seldom went to London, where he was irked to find himself less important than in the north. On one rare visit he fought a duel with an officer of the Lifeguards who had turned back his horses when Lowther had ordered them to break through the line of carriages converging on a court levee. At Lowther he fell passionately in love with 'a fine young girl of humble parentage'[38] and brought her to live at the hall. When she died young he had her embalmed and would go to look at her face through her glass case. In sum he was described as 'a madman too rich to be confined'.[39]

Among his seats was Cockermouth, and it was for this that Brown's son, Lancelot, hoped to be chosen. Also hoping for it, however, was a cousin of Lowther's, Walter Stanhope, the same Yorkshire landowner who commented favourably on Brown's improvements at Alnwick Castle.

'You are come in right time... *we want young men*',[40] Lowther wrote to Stanhope in the autumn of 1774 when Parliament had been dissolved and seats would be vacant. Stanhope arrived at Lowther and pressed his case, but for several months Sir James would not make up his mind, persistently telling Stanhope to stay, cancelling his chaise when he tried to leave, but refusing to give him a definite answer.

'Lounged about all day,' Stanhope wrote in his diary, 'Sir James drenched us in port and Madeira till four in the morning.'[41]

By 5 December he was writing, 'Everybody about him [Lowther] takes it for granted that I shall be one, and Brown, the son of Capability, the other; and I know he has said no more, if so much, to him as to me'.[42] And a fortnight later, by which time Stanhope and Lowther were visiting London, 'What to do, upon my word I know not. Mr Brown is equally uninformed who is the other ostensible man, and goes along down [to Lowther] with us... I lose all patience and begin to wish it was all over and were lost, rather than in this state of tantalization.'[43]

Eventually in mid-January Lancelot was told he was unlucky. Lowther 'has explained himself to Mr Brown, who is now here, and has excused himself from bringing him in; and in my opinion he had greater reason to expect than I have. I may be chosen rather than him, but it is full as possible that I may be disappointed.'[44]

Stanhope *was* disappointed (though a few months later Lowther gave him one of two seats for both of which another of his candidates had been chosen). Lancelot, in spite of this failure, continued to search for a seat, suggesting that he was either no great lawyer or that he found politics more glamorous.

Meanwhile Brown's naval son, John, was now on active service off North America. In the same year, 1775, he wrote home that it was 'beyond conception how well they [the American colonists] are prepar'd all along the coast'.[45] His ship *Nautilus* had been hit by fire from the shore and two men wounded. Brown was worried. In a letter from Yorkshire to his wife, he hoped that 'we shall have better news from New York and poor Jack. Those accounts that came from there last in my opinion are very disagreeable.'[46]

It seems possible that John's danger partly explains Brown's hostility to the American war. There were reasons why he might have supported it. He had, after all, worked for George Grenville, who imposed the original Stamp Duties on the colonists, and he was not only a royal gardener, but a personal friend of George III, whose ministers were pursuing it. Yet in a letter to the Earl of Harcourt he called it 'so unfortunate and disgraceful a war'.[47]

If anxiety about his son is one explanation for his attitude there is another. He was a friend of William Pitt. Throughout his life, from his arrival at Stowe till his death forty-two years later, Brown was on friendly terms with many of the most powerful men in the country. He worked for no fewer than five Prime Ministers: Grafton, Grenville, Bute, Shelburne and Pitt. As a result he was on the whole wise enough to avoid aligning himself with any particular party or politician. Pitt was the exception.

Brown and Pitt had met at Stowe. Pitt (now Lord Chatham) — the cornet who had been picked by Cobham for encouragement, just as he had picked Brown — had been a regular visitor at Stowe when the Cobham clan gathered there in summer, and had ultimately married Cobham's niece, George Grenville's sister, Hester. He shared with Cobham, and half a dozen of Cobham's relations, a keen interest in landscape gardening. If decisions about Stowe in the 1740s were ultimately taken by Cobham himself (then implemented by Brown), Cobham was almost certainly influenced by the comments of friends and relations, Pitt among them.

During the following years Brown and Pitt had remained in contact and their friendship had produced a commission for Brown. Pitt had given him this when a ninety-year-old admirer, Sir William Pynsent, left him the Somerset estate of Burton Pynsent. Pitt was already too gouty or busy to visit the place, but he wanted a memorial built there to mark his gratitude to Pynsent, and asked Brown for a design, which Brown duly submitted. 'I have sent by your steward,' he wrote to Pitt,

> a design for the pillar which I hope will merit your approbation; if there are any parts you disapprove of, we can very easily correct them when I shall have the honour of seeing you. The figure I have put on the pedestal is that of Gratitude, conveying to Posterity the name of Pinsant; which indeed he himself has distinguished and without flattery done in the most effectual manner by making you his heir. On this topic I could say more, but may my silence convey my respect. And that your King and country may be long, very long, very long blessed with your unparalleled abilities will be the constant wish of Sir, your most obliged and most obedient, humble servant...[48]

Brown's sentiments were more real than their eighteenth century formality might suggest. Two years later when he heard that Pitt might go to Burton Pynsent he wrote to Lady Chatham: 'I was most heartily rejoiced to find that Lord Chatham was well enough to move from North End, and that his Lordship and family were set out for Pynsent. I hope in God that his Lordship mended every day, and that you have all had a good journey.

'Pardon my zeal! Pardon my Vanity, but I wish above all things to know [how] my Lord does, and how the pillar pleases his Lordship.'

Brown had already written three times that year to Lady Chatham, each time asking anxiously about Pitt's health. In 1772 he was writing again:'... a report prevails here that Lord Chatham has lately had a very disagreeable symptom touching his health; I am willing to hope such a report is groundless and that the cultivation of it is to answer some sinister purposes. I need not tell your Ladyship my feeling in everything where Lord Chatham's interest or his happiness is concerned...' He sent two more anxious enquiries that year and wrote again when Pitt's health grew worse in 1777.

Pitt was no doubt flattered by Brown's loyalty. Certainly he thought highly of his professional abilities and his honesty, even if he took a slightly mocking attitude to his social climbing. When Lady Stanhope was planning to employ Brown, Pitt wrote to her:

> The chapter of my friend's dignity must not be omitted. He writes Lancelot Brown, Esquire *en titre d'office:* please to consider, he shares the private hours of --- [the King], dines familiarly with his neighbour of Sion [the Duke of Northumberland], and sits down at the tables of all the house of Lords, etc. To be serious, Madam, he is deserving of the regard shown to him; for I know him, upon very long acquaintance, to be an honest man, and of sentiments much above his birth.

An undated letter from Brown to Pitt suggests that Brown's friendship with the Duke of Northumberland may have been special and not arbitrarily picked out by Pitt. In it Brown tells Pitt that the Duke has been 'astonished at his [the Duke's] son being attact in so violent a manner,' presumably by Pitt, and expresses the surprisingly outspoken wish that Pitt 'will be so good as to pay some little civility to his Grace'.

In 1777 Brown again tried to bring Pitt and the Duke together. 'I told his Grace the state of your Lordship's health' he wrote to Pitt 'on which he told me he would immediately wait on your Lordship. When he comes, I hope your Lordship will be well enough to see his Grace. No man more truly devoted to your Lordship's interest than he is.' Pitt's son replied that in principle nothing would give his father more pleasure than a call from the Duke, but that at present he had 'such strong symptoms of the gout about him' that it was impossible.

If Brown would have liked to reconcile Pitt with the Duke of Northumberland, there were other reconciliations he was even more anxious to promote. One was between Pitt and his brother-in-law, George Grenville. Pitt and Grenville were political enemies, Pitt violently opposed to the war against the American colonists, Grenville still its supporter. In the House of Commons Pitt had mimicked Grenville's lugubrious voice, gaining for him the nickname of 'The Gentle Shepherd'. In

1772 Brown wrote to Lady Chatham: 'I wish to see (but I am doubtful I hope too much) your Ladyship's family once more in perfect union, and not see such useful ability split, and I had almost said, devoted to facteous purposes'.

Brown now also began to attempt the more formidable task of reconciling Pitt with the King, who was even more deeply committed to the war. In the same letter he wrote: 'In a conversation I have lately had [with the King] I was heard with attention, I went so far as I durst, upon such tender ground.'

That October (1777) Pitt made what was probably his bitterest attack on the American war, picking in particular on the use the English were making of the Indians with their scalping knives as allies against the colonists. Undaunted, Brown continued to act as Pitt's apologist to the King, and wrote next month to Lady Chatham to report progress.

> … Today, and indeed many opportunities have occurred of late, in which I have had very favourable conversations [with the King]; — no acrimony, nor ill will appeared. I was told, that Lord Chatham was perfectly restored; much conversation arose on the word *restored*. I was then informed, that his Lordship was to come up to oppose the Address for the Speech; I said, that it was very unlike Lord Chatham to declare he would oppose before he knew the subject. I was told the intelligence was from an enemy quarter; but that quarter had it from Lord Camden, or in his channel. I then ventured to repeat what he had seen in your Ladyship's letter, that Lord Chatham was not changed in sentiment; that I was very sure what his Lordship had advanced was meant for the dignity of the crown, the happiness of his Majesty and the royal family, and the lustre of the whole empire; that I had always considered his Lordship in the light of being a friend to the whole, not parts of the empire; that he was a friend to correction, where it was necessary, but that he had rather have the rod kissed than make use of it; that some people had very much injured Lord Chatham in calling him an American, abstracted from the duty of a good English subject; because I knew, after forty years' experience, that no man loved his country more…

The following February Earl Temple passed on to Lady Chatham (his sister) what he described as one of 'a monstrous heap of stories' which were circulating in London, but one which seems entirely credible and probably described Brown's final attempt to act as Pitt's champion. 'Our friend Brown came, the other morning, piping hot from Lord Bute; who was outrageous in his expressions on the indispensable necessity, that the King should not lose a moment in sending for Lord Chatham, and this in terms and with a violence, which convinced him of his Lordship's sincerity and apprehensions.'

Soon afterwards, in April, Pitt collapsed while speaking in the House of Lords. At this point Brown set off for the north. As soon as he was back on 9 May, he wrote to Lady Chatham: 'I am just returned from a long northern expedition on which I have spent many anxious hours, on account of Lord Chatham's health, where however, I had the comfort to find one universal wish that his Lordship's life

67. George III by the studio
of Allan Ramsay, *c.* 1767.

may be preserved to save this devoted sinking country, but alas, I am doubtful it is too far gone even for his Lordship to redeem us.'

Pitt died two days later.

Brown never again intervened in politics, and it is a fair conclusion that only his friendship and admiration for Pitt had ever made him do so. The whole episode could be evidence that Brown had become pleased with himself and tried to meddle where he had no skill or influence. But his actions provide a more interesting insight into his character. They suggest that he was essentially a man who liked to create peace and amiability around him, and that he found disagreements between his special friends and patrons — Pitt, Northumberland, George Grenville and the King, especially distressing.

Here perhaps is the underlying clue to Brown the landscaper as well as Brown the person. The curving lakes and vast sweeps of undulating lawn which he created around the great houses of his patrons produce an atmosphere of benign calm which significantly parallels the sort of friendships with which he wished personally to surround himself.

11. Isis and Cam

IF SIR WILLIAM CHAMBERS'S criticisms of Brown found a number of supporters, they had little effect on Brown's business. No clients left him and many fresh ones wanted him. One who returned for more was Lord Craven, for whom Brown had made the vast and splendid lake at Coombe Abbey near Coventry. Craven now turned his attention to his estate at Benham in Berkshire, and so, as she remembered it in her memoirs, did Lady Craven.

This was a favourite spot with me and Lord Craven, and it gave me infinite pain to see it parted with [by her son]. I had built it myself, with my husband's permission, and laid out the grounds according to my own taste; nor would I suffer any of the modern landscape gardeners to interfere, though strongly pressed to allow them. The famous man called Capability Brown was desirous of being employed but as he had already laid out twelve thousand pounds for Lord Craven at Coombe Abbey, I thought it unnecessary to be more plundered, and trust to myself for adding to nature.[1]

Lady Craven's estimate of Brown's payments is only a little exaggerated. His account book shows that by May 1774 Craven had paid him at least £7,650 9s. But it was his wife's plans rather than Brown's bills that alarmed Craven. In June 1773 he wrote to Brown: 'If you can possibly spare a day next week, I shall be very happy to see you here, as I much wish to know your sentiments respecting this place, particularly the turning of the road. I am more desirous of seeing you soon as Lady Craven wishes to make some alterations here and to begin immediately...'[2]

Brown came, and Craven was protected, for it was Brown and his son-in-law, Henry Holland, who together built him a fine new house at Benham and landscaped the grounds.

Like Bowood, Corsham and Tottenham, the estate lay close to a route which must have been wearyingly familiar to Brown, the Bath Road, but here, in Berkshire, only a few miles beyond Newbury, it had the advantage of following the picturesque valley of the Kennet. As a result Benham had a fine position above the river, which formed an extensive mill pool with an island, stretching from side to

68. Benham House, Berkshire.

side of its southerly view. Brown must have planted around the pool, and perhaps extended it. Typically, the large walled garden was set beyond its upper end at an inconvenient distance.

Most of the work of taking down the old house and building the new one was done in the years 1773 to 1777; in total it cost about £11,000, though Brown only records receiving £7,080. Of the total of about £20,000 which Craven paid or agreed to pay Brown for Coombe Abbey and Benham, some perhaps went direct to Holland, but it is still curious that only £1000 ever passed through Brown's bank account at Drummonds, and provides further evidence of a close friendship between Craven and Brown which enabled Craven to pay in less formal ways.

The house with its magnificent Ionic portico, was later given a third storey, but the original must have been fine enough, the ground floor rooms particularly splendid. After many years of neglect, it is now being conscientiously renovated to become the head office of a commercial company. Today it has a curious connection with Stowe; two particularly elegant fire-places in the hall were brought from Stowe after the sale there in 1922.[3]

In these years, the mid 1770s, Brown also created a garden at Sheffield Place which today has become one of the finest in the south-east of England. His client was John Baker Holroyd, later Earl of Sheffield. In 1777 John Foster wrote to Holroyd, 'I shall not... take up much of your time, which must be agreeably employed between Wyatt, Brown and the farm'.[4] James Wyatt was building a new Gothic house for Holroyd. The farm was one of Holroyd's particular interests; its meticulously kept accounts survive, and he later became first President of the Board of Agriculture. Brown, according to tradition, landscaped the park, and there is other evidence besides Foster's letter to support this claim, but tantalisingly little.

Holroyd had bought Sheffield Place eight years earlier. Apart from his agricultural work, he is best remembered for an incident which was still to come: his dramatic intervention in the events which led to the Gordon Riots. On 2 June 1780, when the Protestant Association presented its petition to Parliament he took hold of Lord George Gordon and told him, 'Hitherto I have imputed your conduct to madness, but now I perceive that it has more of malice than madness in it'. Holroyd (who had already raised at his own expense a regiment in Sussex) personally led a detachment of the troops which suppressed the riot.[5] In private life his closest friend was Gibbon, who wrote parts of *The History of the Decline and Fall of the Roman Empire* in the library at Sheffield Place. Though the dates of Brown's work are uncertain, Gibbon probably watched it in progress, and Brown may well have met Gibbon during one of the visits which his account book records.

It is here, in his account book, that there is firm evidence of his involvement. His assistant, Spyers, came to Sheffield Place in May 1776 and spent a week making 'a small survey... for the alterations of the place particularly for the water and ground about it'. For twelve years now, sending Spyers to make a survey had been one of Brown's standard practices. A plan, a contract and the work then followed, though

69. Part of the series of linked lakes at Sheffield Park, East Sussex.

not often in such a rational order. Unfortunately neither contract nor plans for Sheffield Place by Brown or Spyers survive. What is more, an ornate coloured plan of two years earlier by Bernard Scalé shows that the great water at the eastern side of the park, which is always claimed to be Brown's already existed. Adding to the confusion, another field plan by Scalé of the same date (1774) suggests than an old track still crossed the lake.[6]

It is possible that Brown had been working here earlier, that he was already making this lake but that no records survive. Certainly work in the grounds had begun earlier. Trees were being felled in 1771, when two massive oaks were dragged to Lewes by a team of twenty-four oxen.[7] Scalé's plan shows that formal avenues near the house had already gone, and the park to the south-east of the house is set with clumps which are Brown-like.

On the other hand what may have happened — it can only be a guess — is that Scalé included the water on his more ornate map as a proposal. This map was anyway meant to be ornamental as well as useful. It is oval in shape, shows yachts on the lake and was once hung as a painting. Two years later Brown may have made the lake it proposed. The obvious place for such a great lake was here, filling the shallow valley where the Sheffield Mill Stream bordered the park.

Today Sheffield Park (as the gardens are now called) has two upper lakes which lie in a side valley and descend to Brown's lake. And in the second half of the nineteenth century the Third Earl of Sheffield, as well as adding these and planting many exotic trees, divided Brown's lake into two, placing a dam and cascade between them. At least twice, these have had to be drained and dredged (suggesting that Brown's technology was less effective than usual), the first time by the unemployed after the First World War, the second time after the Second World War when the National Trust bought the gardens.

The Third Earl was a cricket enthusiast as well as a landscape gardener. He arranged for the first Test Match between England and Australia to be played on his cricket ground beyond Brown's lake; and during the long winter of 1890-1891, well-known Sussex cricketers took part in a number of matches which were played on its frozen surface.

70. Sheffield Park. The skyline is now dominated by exotic trees.

In 1777 Brown — and presently Henry Holland — were called to Nuneham Courtenay, a few miles south of Oxford on the banks of the Thames, by the Second Earl of Harcourt. The Nuneham Courtenay which most travellers see today consists of two rows of identical, brick, estate cottages which stand on either side of the main road from Oxford to Wallingford. The old village lay behind these to the west, and Harcourt's grounds were beyond again, still closer to the river.

The family's main residence lay upstream, at Stanton Harcourt, but in 1755 the First Earl was one of the earliest landowners to wish to have a seat with a view. Though he intended at first to build only a villa at Nuneham (to Lady Harcourt's distress) he and his architect, Stiff Leadbetter, gradually expanded the plans. One of their problems was a shortage of stone, for the local Headington quarry was also supplying the Duke of Marlborough. As a result, foundation stone had to be taken from the Stanton Harcourt house and floated down the Thames to Nuneham.

Here Leadbetter set his house in a magnificent position on a bluff, with views down to the river half a mile away, then across a vast expanse of country with the spire of Abingdon Church central against the Berkshire Downs. Further to the right trees (and pylons) now spoil what was once an equally fine view of Oxford's domes and spires.

The First Earl was described by Horace Walpole as 'a marvel of pomposity and propriety'. At court he taught the future George III proper royal behaviour, and he was sent by George in 1761 to be his proxy at Mecklenburg and make the required twelve applications to the future Queen Charlotte before she was allowed to acccept George's offer of marriage. Harcourt retired from active diplomacy in 1777 to the leisure of his country house but only enjoyed it for a few months. 'Lord Harcout was missing t'other day at dinner time,' Walpole wrote, 'at last he was found suffocated in a well with his head downwards... an odd exit for the Governor of a King, an Ambassador and Viceroy.'[8] Harcourt had been trying to rescue his small dog.

Meanwhile he had had the old village moved from his grounds and its occupants rehoused in the new one already mentioned. This was the event which probably inspired Goldsmith's 'The Deserted Village'. Though Brown was not responsible for moving Nuneham Courtenay, village removal was a process in which he played his part elsewhere, and the new village at Nuneham could well have been an inspiration for the estate village he was currently supervising at Milton Abbas, which in its general layout is strikingly similar.

The village removed, the First Earl had built a classical church on a hilltop on the site of the demolished mediaeval church. Here it functioned chiefly as a garden ornament since it was much too far from the transported villagers to be their place of worship. It had even finer views than the house. Walpole considered it the garden's principal feature, 'worthy of entombing Abelard and Heloisa'.[9]

The Second Earl was, predictably, in revolt against his pompous father. Before he inherited Nuneham Courtenay he wrote: 'I could not wish my greatest enemy worse, than that he might possess a title, a large acquaintance and a place in the country celebrated for its beauty, that in other words he might be flattered and cheated and be at the mercy of every fool and idler'. He would infuriate his father by retreating to the woods to read Rousseau, coming back late for dinner, 'denouncing hereditary aristocracy, and refusing to be called My Lord'.[10] In 1766 it is thought that he even brought Rousseau to stay in a cottage at Nuneham.

It is therefore somewhat surprising that in 1777, the year he inherited Nuneham, Harcourt should have turned to such an establishment figure as Brown. He was himself a keen gardener and had already, in his father's time, been allowed an acre of ground where he had employed William Mason to create a small, heart-shaped, flower garden. Possibly he was conscious of his own lapse from his principles in using Brown, and this explains his impulse to tease him. In 1779 he wrote to Mason, whom he was still consulting, asking Mason to be present on one such occasion.

Mason declined. 'I see plainly from your Lordship's letter that you wish me to be at Nuneham when Brown is there, that relying on my conciliatory and soothing arts, you may have the pleasure of putting him out of humour every moment and of treating him *en grand seigneur*, and yet for all that get all the good you can out of him, through the medium of my *politesse*.'[11]

Mason may have missed the point, for the real plan was probably to set Brown and Mason at each other. This was certainly what William Whitehead, the Poet Laureate and Harcourt's one-time tutor, suggested. He wrote to Harcourt: 'I long to have Brown find fault with some trifle or other in Mason's alterations; your Lordship must tell him [Mason] when you write that he [Brown] has done so, and it would not come amiss to magnify it a little... I will undertake Mason's defence afterwards for I will not suffer him to be run down'.[12]

None of this, however, should be taken too seriously. Whitehead and Harcourt regularly wrote to each other in such vein, and although there were underlying differences in the gardening ideas of Mason and Brown (see page 153), Mason admired Brown's park landscapes, and they cooperated at Nuneham without serious differences. Harcourt by implication confirmed this. 'Earl Harcourt,' Humphry Repton wrote, 'although possessing great good taste, gives the whole merit of this garden to Mason the poet, as he does of his pleasure grounds to Brown.'[13]

Brown had as usual been delayed. In the hot summer of 1778 he wrote from Burghley: 'I fully intended to have had the honor of waiting on your Lordship before this time but I was prevented by two causes. One was that of illness, ... being with that and business, and the addition of hot weather totally exhausted; the other was that I had not a man to spare at that time to have put into execution anything we might determine.'[14] The next year, however, he produced his plan.

It was a relatively simple one. There was no need to provide water, since the Thames was there, and the house stood too high for any peripheral belt of trees to enclose its grounds, even if this had been wanted. Instead, Brown suggested thinning the trees on the rising ground between the house and the new church, and on the opposite side of the house, where there had been no garden before but there

71. The rustic bridge and thatched cottage beside the Thames at Nuneham, Oxfordshire.

was something of a natural amphitheatre, an area of dense plantations.

The pathway close to the house which leads to these plantations and is known today as Brown's Walk, is not at all clearly shown on his plan. Beyond, however, where the plan shows it winding through denser trees, it forms the best surviving of his features: the Riverside Walk, with its carefully devised 'peeps' of a rustic bridge, a thatched cottage and the Thames.

The walk led to Lock's Wood and beyond to Lock's Hill, where a ruined castle was planned but never built. Four years after Brown's death, Harcourt was offered the old Carfax conduit, a drinking fountain which had stood at the centre of Oxford, and used it here instead of the castle. Here it still stands against a belt of ancient oaks.

Meanwhile Brown and Holland did major work on the house — though not until 1781, when the American War was over and such extravagance was considered proper. Their relative shares are suggested by payment of £1700 to Brown and £700 to Holland. They must certainly have been paid more since 'Nuneham was literally torn to pieces in the remodelling'.[15] Harcourt wrote to Walpole that he was 'sitting on a rafter, dining out of a hod of mortar'.[16] The wings were given a third storey and the kitchens and servants' hall moved from the ground floor to a new

72. The Carfax conduit standing in Brown's landscape at Nuneham.

courtyard of offices. Fanny Burney, who came here a few years later (August 1786) as lady-in-waiting to the Queen has left a vivid account of her visit. For a quarter of an hour she was lost in the passages of the newly converted ground floor. The house was 'straggling, half-new, half-old, half-comfortable, half-forlorn, begun in one generation and finished in another'. Eventually she was served tea in a garden room, where she waited for the King and Queen to complete their viewing of the park. But confusions continued for the rest of the day and left her too indignant even to mention Brown's landscape.[17]

Walpole however approved. Six months after Brown's death, he wrote: 'I made a visit to Lord and Lady Harcourt, and was much pleased with poor Browne's alteration of the house, and improvements of the place, as much as I could see of them, for there was such a tempest during the two days and half that I was there, that I could not stir out of the house but for one hour'.[18] On another occasion he wrote to Mason to say of Nuneham that he did not know the paradise on earth that he preferred.[19]

The rebuilding of Nuneham had still not begun when Brown became involved with

XXIX. (Above) and XXX. (Overleaf) Sheffield Park, East Sussex.

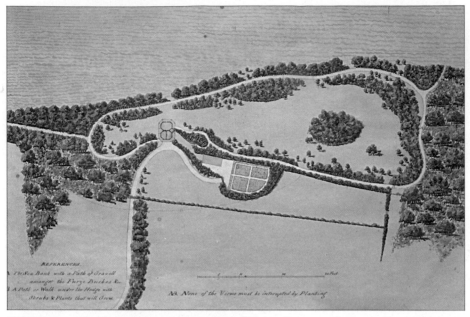

XXXI. Brown's plan for the grounds of the Fishing Cottage, Cadland, Hampshire.

XXXII. Nuneham, Oxfordshire.

a plan for Cambridge far more ambitious than his creation of the Fellows' Garden at St John's, which, if it had been adopted, would have transformed the University's best known landscape feature: the Backs. Who suggested this is not recorded, but it seems a fair guess that the idea was put to the senate by his friends, Dr Powell and Professor Mainwaring. Brown presented his plan in 1779. It was large in scale and revolutionary in concept.

As described by George Dyer, historian of the University, it 'proposed that the river, instead of taking its course, as it comes from Newnham, should be removed to a greater distance from the colleges...; and particularly, instead of moving closely under the western building of St John's, it was, by being moved to a considerable distance, to have taken its course not, as now, on the south side of Magdalen College, but on the north side, between that college and St Peter's Church.'[20]

At least one fellow of St John's, Mr Ashby, considered that 'the expense would have been scarce worth mentioning; a noble young Duke, then residing in one of the colleges, having proposed to set it on foot, by a subscription of £1000'.[21] Dyer fails to mention the feature of Brown's plan which made certain that it would never be accepted. Beyond the Cam the private gardens of the colleges from Peterhouse to Magdalene were to be united into a single park-like area, enclosed by a belt of trees and liberally set with about a dozen clumps. Inevitably the various colleges refused to surrender their privacy and the plan was rejected.

It seems doubtful whether Brown was ever paid for it. Instead, the senate, like St John's, voted him a piece of silver. This tray, bearing the University's arms and inscribed *Ex dono de Academiae Cantabrigiensis A.D. MDCCLXXX*, is now in a private collection,[22] but Brown's plan is preserved at the University Library.

About Wynnstay, the estate of Sir Watkins Williams-Wynn at Ruabon in North Wales, John Byng wrote that it was 'the last work of my friend Lancelot Brown'.[23] Though Byng was right in the sense that Brown left Wynnstay unfinished, by the time he died he had been working there for at least six years, and had been expected to come down and superintend the works as early as 1769.[24]

This was the year when Wynn, still only nineteen, returned from the Grand Tour, and before he married his second wife, Charlotte Grenville, daughter of George Grenville, in 1771. He would then have known of Brown's splendid transformation of Wotton for his father-in-law and have had even better reasons for wanting to employ him.

To friends and acquaintances Wynn seemed a handsome and cultured young man. 'I have yet to see a more aristocratic-looking person,' wrote his neighbour, C.J. Apperley, 'his attire is of the neatest possible description: a light pepper-and-salt mixture coat, a white dimity waistcoat, silk stockings, and, although he never mounted a horse — it may be because his father broke his neck from the back of one — topboots...'[25] He spent much of his time in London, where he was Member of Parliament for Shropshire then Denbighshire, and patronized such well known painters as Reynolds and Dance, but he was keenly interested in improving Wynnstay, commissioning Robert Adam to do many drawings, some for internal features, others for an entirely new house, and employing several gardeners besides Brown, these once again including Richard Woods of Essex. To Apperley, it must have seemed that Wynn could well afford such expenditure, for he estimated his income at £32,000 a year.

If this was ever correct it certainly ceased to be once Wynn had built himself an extravagant new London house in St James's Square. By 1776, a year before Brown finally came to Wynnstay, there was already a *second* plan for selling some of Wynn's estates to rescue him from his debts. From then onwards Wynn wrote continual letters to his agent, Francis Chambre, at Oswestry, imploring him to send money. In increasingly desperate attempts to meet these demands, Chambre raised the rents of Wynn's tenants, in March 1777 having one of them imprisoned for failing to pay or leave.

The same April, Wynn wrote to Chambre: 'I hope that you intend to send me some money soon or I shall be quite broken down'. In December 1779 his 'privy purse' was 'quite *out*... I must desire when you send back the bearer that he may bring with him 100 guineas. I can not do without 50.' In June 1781 he was 'in a more awkward situation than any man of my property ever was before. I have not now 50 guineas in the house nor can I stir because I have not the money to pay for post horses for godsake realise.'[26]

Alongside pleas for money, of which these are only a tiny sample, Wynn wrote regularly to implore Chambre to pay the wages of his labourers. In February 1777 he was 'very much surprised to find... that my various workmen at Wynnstay have been six weeks without wages... There is nothing I hate so much as poor labourers not being payed and nothing brings so much *discredit* to a man...' In August 1779 he hoped that Chambre would 'think of the workmen and people at Wynnstay for I can not stand it if I am to meet fresh complaints there'. And in September 1780 he hoped that he might 'depend on your doing *something* for Salisbury [the steward] for it will be shocking for the workmen to tell at my election what is owing to them'.

Sometimes Wynn tried to reduce his workforce. In April 1778 he proposed to 'speak to Mr Brown when I see him for I am certain 6 men can do his business'. In June 1799 he 'would not have Midgley (the same Midgley whom Brown had employed at Castle Ashby) employ more than 12 men or 18 at most.' But at the same time he would write demanding money for some fresh extravagance: a new town villa or, as in June 1778, a piece of land which Brown needed. 'Since I saw you I have thought and spoken to my wife about Shenriche [?] Farm and I now positively tell you that I *must* have it as I can not make any improvements nor ever live at Wynnstay without it... Mr Brown says he can not make an approach without that ground. My head was thinking of other things yesterday or else I ought to have repeated it to you.'

Chambre grew more and more desperate, eventually drawing up a schedule which showed that, over the six years 1773 to 1778, Wynn had had no more than an average net income of about £4,800, sinking to an actual loss in 1778. When this failed to impress Wynn, he wrote to John Maddocks, a friend of Wynn's: 'I was in hopes after my accounts had been inspected by you, Sir Watkins would have been so far convinced as not to have expected any more impossibilities from me, but I am sorry to inform you that... he still continues to harass me...', and asking Maddocks to 'prevail upon Sir Watkins to make proper allowance for the unexampled slavery I at present undergo for unless he does I can not sustain the weight'.

Meanwhile Brown had come at least five times to Wynnstay.[27] Here he found an upper lake close to the house, perhaps made by Woods. It was later described by Byng as 'a large, straight, ill looking piece of water which being brought there by bad taste, I should think it good taste to destroy'. Fortunately it survives and has matured well. This was probably the 'water and ground about it' for which Brown drew one of his early plans. Certainly Wynn at first required him to work close to the house, outside the windows of the Great Room, or in the pleasure grounds. But to judge by the quantity of trees which were being bought he also probably began to plant in the valley of the Belan, the small tributary of the Dee which ran through the grounds further west. In April 1778 Wynn was furious with Spachman (the gardener) for buying a thousand Spanish chestnuts at £5 a hundred to finish the plantations made that spring, telling Chambre to 'scold Spachman for he deserves it very much'.

Perhaps Wynn's money affairs temporarily improved in 1782 for he wrote to Chambre in May: 'The bills are all settled and we want now only the means of finishing them for which reason I wish you would bring tomorrow 6 or 700... the earlier you can come after 9 tomorrow the better as we expect some of the tradesmen *immediately* after breakfast'. It was in August that year that Wynn paid Brown £300, the only sum Brown ever recorded receiving from him (though the account was settled with Brown's executors after his death). And it could well be that this was when Brown was allowed to begin work on a far more extensive (and no doubt expensive) improvement: the transforming of the deep and dramatic Belan valley into a series of rocky cascades leading to 'a very fine piece of water', to be held up by 'a great dam'.[28]

Brown died before this lake could be completed, and by the time Byng was at Wynnstay in 1784 it was being made in a modified form by one of his assistants,[29] doubtless Midgley. But later the same year a Llwyn-y-groes surveyor, John Evans, carried it out in its full magnificence.

The ceremony which Wynn organized for its opening was of such grandeur that it might have been devised as a memorial tribute to the whole of Brown's work. Led by the gamekeeper and two bagpipers, it included 80 colliers, 100 carters, 200 labourers, 20 artificers, 150 gentlemen and farmers (who had helped with their carts) one wagon with a large piece of roast beef, another with a hogshead of beer with a banner 'TO MOISTEN THE CLAY', Sir Watkins and Lady Williams-Wynn and their daughter in a phaeton drawn by six ponies, Mr Evans on horseback and Mr Midgley with his levelling staff.[30]

The late HENRY HOLLAND, Esq.

View Hans Place.

73. Henry Holland the younger, Brown's partner and son-in-law, by Opie.

12. The Last Years

PERHAPS it was appropriate that Brown, the one-time garden boy who had become a wealthy landed gentleman, should be involved during his last years with two commissions for his banker, Robert Drummond.

Drummonds Bank had been founded in 1717 by Andrew Drummond, an enterprising Scot, and he remained a partner till he died in 1769. By this time it had survived a number of financial crises and was growing prosperous, in particular by handling the pay of the army of 10,000 which George III was keeping in the American colonies. It was used not only by the King, but by a remarkable number of rich and influential men of the times. In 1765 it had on its books the accounts of six dukes, forty-three peers and forty-two other titled persons.[1] Surprisingly, since none of the Drummonds of the time seem to have cared much about the arts, it was also used by architects, painters and musicians, including Gibbs, the brothers James and Robert Adam, and Sir William Chambers. Many of the clients of the bank were also Brown's clients, and could have recommended it to him, but the suggestion could also have come from another of the bank's customers, Henry Holland, the elder.

The records of Brown's dealings with the bank are of much interest, often confirming that he was working on particular gardens in particular years.[2] And though today they seem curiously incomplete because his own private account book shows numerous payments which never passed through his bank but were presumably received in cash or notes of hand, they also show that he worked at certain gardens about which no other records survive.

Unfortunately they do not help to solve the problem of whether or not the Mr Drummond who, in 1767, had made an offer for the manor which Brown eventually bought was one of the partners of the bank, but, as I have suggested above, he was probably Henry Drummond. It could also have been his brother Robert. Both were nephews of the founder, Andrew. Uncle Andrew had by this time retired to his own fine property at Stanmore, Middlesex — where he was described as a 'sort of Roger der Coverley... living in great style which he could well afford... very vain of his place, which he got Capability Brown to dress up'[3] — and his two nephews were effectively running the bank.

They belonged to a dining club known as 'the gang', and letters between its twelve members give glimpses of the character of Robert Drummond, the brother with whom Brown became most involved. He was notorious for his obsession with fishing, and commonly referred to as 'Fisherman Bob', or 'Our friend Piscador'. As the senior partner he was also 'Governor Bob', and he lived at Charing Cross, close to the bank. Here, in April 1773, his house caught fire. 'The alarm was so sudden and so serious, that when the children were collected and... having secured their persons, they began to think of their effects. Tatty [Mrs Drummond] sent with much anxiety for a drawer, containing letters of one Keith; and Bob soon after appeared, bringing into the place of safety, not his papers nor his plate, but a fishing-rod and a box of his choicest flies...'[4]

Tatty was Winifred Thompson, an illegitimate daughter of Berkeley Lucy of Charlecote, who thus gave Brown another connection with Robert, for she was the half-sister of his client there, George Lucy.

Robert Drummond now bought himself his own country property, near Cadland Creek, between the New Forest and Southampton Water. It had no great house, and for three years he would stay at farms on the estate, using it merely for fishing and snipe shooting. Then, in 1775, he engaged Brown and Holland to build a house and to landscape the grounds. Drummond is said to have spent a total of £75,000 on Cadland. By 1778 Brown's share amounted to £12,500 — though with typical scrupulousness he wrote to Robert Drummond to say that he had been overpaid. 'On looking over the accounts I find you added for my trouble on the out of doors work, two hundred pounds, which is more than I can possibly accept of you, by one hundred pounds.'[5]

Brown and Holland seem to have satisfied Drummond, and the house and grounds were admired by discerning visitors. The Revd William Gilpin, rector of Boldre a few miles inland from Cadland and author of many books on the Picturesque, wrote that 'the abundance of old timber gives the house, though lately built, so much the air and dignity of an ancient mansion that Mr Brown, the ingenious improver of it, used to say "It was the oldest new place he knew in England"'.[6]

Holland's plan for the house and Brown's for the grounds survive.[7] So does an engraving which shows a modest mansion of five bays, built, like Claremont, in white brick, but with no great flight of steps or Palladian entrance, surrounded by the woodland which gave it its long-established atmosphere. House and woodland have disappeared below Fawley Refinery.

They must have pleased Drummond, for a few years later he gave Brown and Holland their second commission: to improve a small nearby property which lay a couple of miles to the south-east, on the banks, not of Southampton Water like Cadland, but of the Solent, with views across this to the Isle of Wight. Here Holland designed one of the earliest *cottages ornés* consisting of a pair of thatched octagons, to be called the Fishing Cottage, and Brown laid out a garden which in a

74. Old Scots pines at Cadland, Hampshire.

unique way compressed into seven acres many of the features of his grander parks. For the cottage garden he presented one of his more decorative plans, possibly drawn by himself then coloured and ornamented by Spyers. It could have been meant as something special for his fisherman banker.

It was inscribed:

'A. The sea bank with a path of gravell amongst the furze bushes, etc;

B. A path or walk under the hedge with shrubs and plants that will grow.

N.B. None of the views must be interrupted by planting.'

The views, as might be expected, were his main concern. 'Furze bushes etc', and 'shrubs and plants that will grow', are hardly the instructions of a plantsman.

To conclude the story of the Fishing Cottage, two years after Brown's death, the Drummonds were visiting it one fine summer day when it was burned to the ground. 'A party of gentlemen were assembled to dinner there', *The Morning Chronicle and London Advertiser* reported, 'when about three o'clock, smoke was observed to issue from the building, and in less than an hour it was consumed. The furniture was happily saved; the company sat down after the accident to a fine haunch of venison, and the remains of the dinner and some excellent wines, helped to dissipate the gloom of the day. It is supposed the fire kindled from sparks of the kitchen fire falling on the thatch of the cottage.'[8]

During the blaze Robert Drummond had been missed but all was well. He was rescuing the wine from the cottage's cellar.

75. Cadland: view from the garden of the Fishing Cottage, across the Solent to the Isle of Wight.

The cottage was rebuilt, destroyed again by fire in 1916, and finally replaced in the 1930s by a modest mansion in white brick with bow windows and a tall, steeply pitched, tiled roof. Meanwhile, and for a further forty years, the planting around the house was allowed to thicken and spread till it obscured not only the Solent and the Isle of Wight but every other vista or effect which Brown had intended.

During the last few years the Drummonds — it is now their main residence, renamed Cadland House — in a remarkable feat of restoration, have remade Brown's miniature park. Below the tangled woodland of self-seeded Scots pine and invasive sycamore with its undergrowth of brambles and bracken they found intact 'the bones of the garden'. Some of the larger trees, even some of the pines which make slow growth in the sandy soil here, were probably Brown's. The gravel walks, which reappeared from below two hundred years of woodland debris, certainly were. Closer to the house the lawns have been cleared and resown, so that the surrounding belt of trees is again clearly defined, with Brown's clump at its centre, and a break re-opened to allow the view of the Isle of Wight which Brown intended, with Ryde church steeple as a distant eye-catcher. In due course the small 'vegetable garden' which stands on its own to the north-west, will also be replanted. It was too small and too far from the main house ever to have been planned as a serious vegetable garden, and was perhaps where the ladies picked flowers while the men finished their picnic claret.

The Drummonds, in their attempts to recreate precisely Brown's garden, have rooted out plants known to have been later imports and replaced them with ground cover which he would have used: laurel, *Rhododendron ponticum*, butcher's broom and roses. Philip Miller's plant list for a wilderness of fourteen years earlier provides some evidence of what was available. So does Brown's plant list for Petworth of the late 1750s. But these are conservative guides in a period when new species were arriving all the time.

Like a Kent garden, Cadland's should be toured by the correct route, to experience the desired sequence of impressions. Sometimes the banks of the perimeter walk rise to enclose the path, sometimes they fall away to give a feeling of liberation, periodically they provide peepholes with views of the Solent, not unlike the 'peeps' of the Thames which Brown had made a few years earlier at Nuneham Courtenay. The final effect is to create in a small space a garden of so many changing moods and surprises that it seems a great deal larger than it is, and regularly confuses the visitor about its size and shape.

In other ways the year 1782 was not, for Brown, greatly different from those immediately before. He continued to live mainly in Wilderness House, with occasional visits to his manor at Fenstanton. When he was in London he stayed with his elder daughter, now Bridget Holland, in Hertford Street.

Still living with the Browns at home was their other daughter, Margaret, now in her early thirties. Brown was particularly fond of Margaret, calling her Peggy and sending her letters when he was on his travels. In one of these he calls her 'the daughter that I dearly love'. Peggy in turn was fond of her father. She saved the letters he wrote to her and made an important collection of other letters connected with her father's work which tell us many things about him that would otherwise not be known.[9] During the previous few years Peggy had become engaged to a Mr Gee. Brown and his wife seem to have approved of this young man. Certainly when, in January 1782, Peggy wrote to tell Brown that she was no longer sure she wanted to marry him, Brown's answer was not that of a relieved father who welcomes the end of a mistaken infatuation. On the contrary, he asked her to consider Mr Gee's feelings. 'He you have made miserable and if this thing goes off you will be much blamed... I on comparing all things together hope you will find that the best thing you can do is to marry Mr Gee... Remember my Dear Child that I lay no commands, that my wish is your happiness which that you may be is the ardent prayer of, dear, dear Peggy, your affectionate father.'[10] Peggy broke off her engagement, and Brown did not live to see her married.

Meanwhile his middle son, John, *had* married. His naval career prospered and he eventually became an Admiral of the Blue. And Brown's eldest son, Lance, had at last entered Parliament, where he represented Totnes. Later Brown's country neighbour, the Earl of Sandwich, twice got Lance elected for Huntingdon, but he was never a successful politician and the highest position he ever held was Gentleman of the King's Privy Chamber. Brown's last child, Thomas, went into the church.

In 1782, as in previous years, Brown journeyed actively about the country.

Cadland was only one place where he needed to supervise work commissioned in previous years. At Nuneham Courtenay the rebuilding of the house had only begun in 1781. And though Brown was no longer receiving regular payments from Burghley, it was in 1781 and 1782 that he sent plans for the staircase to Verrio's painted rooms in an unsuccessful bid for new work there. In East Anglia he sent a second plan to Sir Gerard Vanneck of Heveningham, where work had begun the previous year. In the Cotswolds he visited Lord Ducie Morton at Woodchester Park, once more sending Spyers to make a plan. And he made at least one visit to Wynnstay in North Wales.

By October he was in Yorkshire, making a preliminary visit to Sir John Ramsden at Byram, where he hoped for a new commission. The weather had been exceptionally bad. Walpole noted that the Thames was as full and fast flowing as the Rhone,[11] and Brown wrote that 'the season has been such as I never saw before'.[12]

These words were part of a letter to Elizabeth Montagu, mistress of Sandleford Priory, just south of Newbury in Berkshire. She was one of the original Blue Stocking ladies, who had once been married, but hoped in future that she would 'escape the matrimonial influenza'.[13] Nevertheless, she had inherited a comfortable fortune from her husband, who had owned coal mines. This enabled her in five years to spend £36,000 'as successfully as if I was Esquire instead of Madam' on land, on a new town house by 'Athenian' Stuart, on extensive alterations by James Wyatt to Sandleford Priory and on improvements to its grounds by Brown.

She and Brown corresponded, and enjoyed each other's letters. To her sister-in-law she wrote: 'I am very glad Mr Brown likes me as a correspondent'. Though Brown's letters were not exactly intimate, they were a shade less formal than usual. 'I was honoured with your letter,' he wrote, 'which is an exact picture of your mind, full of compassion and good will to all... Your sister does me honour in mentioning me.'[14]

When Brown visited Sandleford, Mrs Montagu found him 'an agreeable, pleasant companion as well as a great genius in his profession. I consider him a great poet.' And though she thought that he must find her a modest employer she wrote that he gave 'the poor widow and her paltry plans as great attention as he could bestow on an unlimited commission and an unbounded space'. Furthermore the work was to be spread out, enabling her to 'execute as much of it every year as I choose'.

Brown was 'to lead the view from the east window of the eating room' and there create an 'arched roof of twilight groves'. Wyatt's new eating room, which he had made by putting a false ceiling below the astonishing timbered roof of the ancient chapel, so charmed her that mutton eaten there tasted like venison and she was sure that 'all my geese will be swans, when Mr Brown has improved the little river which divides Admiral Derby's territory and mine'.

By July 1782, twenty men were at work 'in the wood and grove' and she gave a supper 'for all the work-people employed under the direction of Mr Brown in

76. Sandleford Priory, Berkshire.

adorning and embellishing the pleasure ground. The appetite with which they eat, the jollity with which they laughed and sung showed me I had not ill bestowed my meat and drink.' They were unemployed weavers from Newbury who were 'not dextrous at the rake and pitchfork, but the plain digging and driving wheel barrows they can perform and are very glad to get their daily subsistence'.

To supervise the work Brown employed as head gardener a boxer and reformed alcoholic who became a religious maniac. He gave no trouble while Brown was alive but later Mrs Montagu wrote that 'while he was ordering the workmen how to apply their spades, he fell on his knees and muttered prayers; he is now so wild I know not what to do with him. I am going to write to Mr Lapidge, who is to finish [what] Mr Brown began, to come with all speed to take care of this poor creature; in the meantime I dare not walk about the grounds... In his religious enthusiasm he fancies he must atone for past offences and it has been difficult to persuade him to sleep in a house, and he has endeavoured to eat grass.'[15] When men eventually came to take him to St Luke's or Bedlam, he broke loose and despite a search for miles around, was not recaptured.

Today Sandleford Priory is a girls' school, Wyatt's eating room their gymnasium and Brown's planting reduced to a few stunted cedars, a couple of fine oaks and a derelict Spanish chestnut. But the lake which the weavers of Newbury expanded survives, backed by magnificent rhododendrons of later date; and there are plans for new tree planting in Brown's style which may one day recreate his 'twilight groves'.

In January 1783 Brown set out once more from Hampton Court, now for Euston Hall, the Suffolk seat of the Duke of Grafton. By chance this, Brown's final journey, epitomizes important features of his life and work: the wealth and power of his clients (Grafton had become George III's Prime Minister in 1776), and the way in which he left them so satisfied that they frequently came back to him again (he had made the large lake for Grafton's lodge at Wakefield while he was still at Stowe in the 1740s).

On 5 February Brown was back in London, staying with his married daughter. On this day he added a codicil to his will. It merely made alterations to small legacies which he had previously intended for his brother George's children, but is interesting that he should have chosen this day to add it. The will itself he had made four years earlier. It left his wife, besides his coach and three horses, an annuity of £400, an outright sum of £1,000 and most of his other possessions. To his children he left sums varying from £7,000 (Lancelot), to £1,000 (Bridget).[16]

Next evening he went to dine with Lord Coventry. Again by chance his final social engagement epitomizes one of the most characteristic features of his life: the way in which his aristocratic clients became and remained his personal friends. For Coventry he had carried out what was probably his first landscaping commission after Cobham's death, and had built Croome Court, his first country mansion. He returned from dinner after dark, reached Hertford Street about 9 o'clock, collapsed on his daughter's doorstep and died at once. He was sixty-seven years old. Accounts agree that he fell heavily, and some suggest that it was from his fall that he died, but it seems a better guess that he suffered a fatal stroke or heart attack.

'Your dryads must go into black gloves, Madam,' Walpole wrote to Lady Ossory: 'their father-in-law, Lady Nature's second husband, is dead! Mr Brown dropped down at his door yesterday.'[17] To Mason he wrote: 'I made a bad epitaph for him which if you please you may recolour...

> With one lost Paradise the name
>   Of our first ancestor is stained;
> Brown shall enjoy unsullied fame
>   For many a Paradise regained.[18]

Brown died when his reputation was still at its height. Even the adverse criticism generated by Chambers and his supporters ten years earlier had died down. There were a number of formal eulogies in prose and verse, and only one known expression of mixed feelings. Mason reported this to Walpole. 'Soon after the news of Brown's death had reached the r...l ear [the King's] he went over to Richmond gardens and in a tone of great satisfaction said to the under-gardener: "Brown is dead! Now Mellicent *you* and *I* can do *here* what we please".'[19] Walpole replied: 'Your story on Brown's death is worth a million'.[20]

But Walpole remained a defender of Brown's reputation and came to his support

77. Bridget Holland, Brown's
daughter. (By courtesy of
Sotheby's.)

when, ten years later, Richard Payne Knight, a leader of the Picturesque movement, attacked him.

> Hence, hence! thou haggard fiend, however called,
> Thin, meagre genius of the bare and bald
> Thy spade and mattock, here at length lay down
> Thy fav'rite Brown, whose innovating hand
> First dealt thy curses o'er this fertile land.[21]

'The abuse of Brown is as coarse and illiberal as it is cruel and unjust,' Walpole
wrote.[22]

Uvedale Price, a squire from Herefordshire, had a personal reason for attacking
Brown's style of landscaping, which he did about the same time.

I may perhaps have spoken more feelingly on this subject from having done
myself what I so condemn in others, — destroyed an old fashioned garden. It
was not indeed in the high style of those I have described, but it had many of the
same circumstances, and had their effect. As I have long since perceived the
advantage which I could have made of them, and how much I could have added
to that effect; how well I could in parts have mixed the modern style, and have
altered and concealed many of the stiff and glaring formalities, I have long
regretted its destruction.[23]

At the time of Brown's death, Walpole pasted into his notebook an anonymous obituary which included a phrase that has provided a text for modern critics of his work. 'Such, however, was the effect of his genius that when he was the happiest man, he will be least remembered; so closely did he copy nature that his works will be mistaken.' It would be easy to name a dozen of his landscapes, from his very earliest at Kiddington, Oxfordshire, to the Grecian Valley at Stowe, to Grimsthorpe in Lincolnshire, where today this indeed seems to be true. The claim that the trees of such landscapes have now reached their full maturity points precisely to the quality which makes them today seem part of nature rather than an inspired transformation of it.

Nature has closed carriageways, produced beds of reeds at lake edges and caused the collapse of garden buildings. Relatively few of Brown's parks have been preserved in the way eighteenth century labour would have kept them. In even fewer have his tree clumps or belts been replanted. The two-hundred-year-old trees which are original have their own fascination. Ours will be the last generation to see the surviving beeches, and all but a very few of the Scots pines have already gone. And though it can be shown, as at Blenheim, that the longer-lived oaks and Spanish chestnuts seldom even now obscure the vistas they were planned to frame, they bear little resemblance to the elegant trees of so many contemporary prints and paintings. It is these, surely, which best illustrate Brown's ideal.

It is difficult to do more than suggest this ideal, let alone define the theory which lay behind it, because Brown said so little to explain, let alone justify himself. But a letter he wrote in 1775 to the Revd Thomas Dyer suggests that he did have a theory, and that what might be called a light touch in tree planting was a key part of it. To produce 'all the elegance and all the comforts which mankind wants in the country', Brown wrote, required not only 'a good plan, good execution, a perfect knowledge of the country and the objects in it', but 'infinite delicacy in the planting etc., so much beauty depending on the size of the trees and the colour of their leaves to produce the effect of light and shade so very essential to the perfecting of a good plan.'[24]

Brown's remarks to Hannah More, the well known lady of letters, herself a gardener, have been more often quoted, and perhaps given too much significance. He met the old lady one day at Hampton Court, strolling in the palace grounds, during the last few months of his life. 'I took a very agreeable lecture from him in his art,' she wrote,'... He illustrates everything he says about gardening by some literary or grammatical allusion... He told me he compared his art to literary composition. "Now *there*," he said, pointing his finger, "I make a comma, and there," pointing to another spot, "where a more decided turn is proper, I make a colon; at another part, where an interruption is desirable to break the view, a parenthesis; now a full stop, and then I begin another subject."'[25]

Brown was of course being modest, but behind his words lay the philosophical idea on which his work had always been based: that nature tended towards the ideal and that the gardener's duty was merely to correct her accidents. He was also, no doubt, translating his own technique into Miss More's literary terms. For this reason it seems unwise to take his words too literally. Though breaks in tree planting can easily be seen as stops or colons, a great stretch of water — the principal feature of the majority of his landscapes — cannot very usefully be compared to a punctuation mark.

As for Brown himself, there is not the smallest doubt that he was a phenomenon. With the possible exception of Le Nôtre, no landscape gardener in any country in any age has stood out so singularly as the representative of what was almost universally agreed to be best. And if the scale on which he worked in part explains our amazement at what he did, the number of his buildings and landscapes is equally astonishing.

It is easy to explain him away as the product of his age. Social and economic historians may suggest that if he had not lived, it would have been necessary to invent him. Certainly many things came together at this time to make his success possible, some technical, some economic, some social. Walpole was undoubtedly right to suggest that the most important technical invention was the ha-ha, which allowed the uniting of the garden with the countryside beyond. It was a short step then to bring the 'naturalness' of the countryside *into* the garden. And this, to speak in the broadest terms, seemed desirable because nature was no longer threatening or alarming, as it had seemed in earlier times.

And the period in which Brown worked was one in which the ruling families of England had grown phenomenally rich, so that they could afford the huge water works and the taking out of cultivation of many acres of land which the making of vast, unproductive parks required. Distancing themselves from the common people with belts of trees and extensive lawns, and sweeping villages into the distance was a natural accompaniment to the sense of security which such prosperity brought with it. To suggest that Brown *imposed* on his clients changes of this sort is absurd.

What all this fails to explain is why Brown, from a fairly large number of landscape gardeners of the time, rose to stand alone. The individual qualities which brought him his success are not too difficult to list. He was scrupulously honest. He worked phenomenally hard. He had precisely the right manner with his patrons: respectful but authoritative. He was bold, advanced and inventive in using new landscaping techniques. Above all, he had a marvellous eye for seeing in a landscape as it existed what could be made of it. But it was the combination of these qualities in a single person which made him famous in his time and a genius in retrospect.

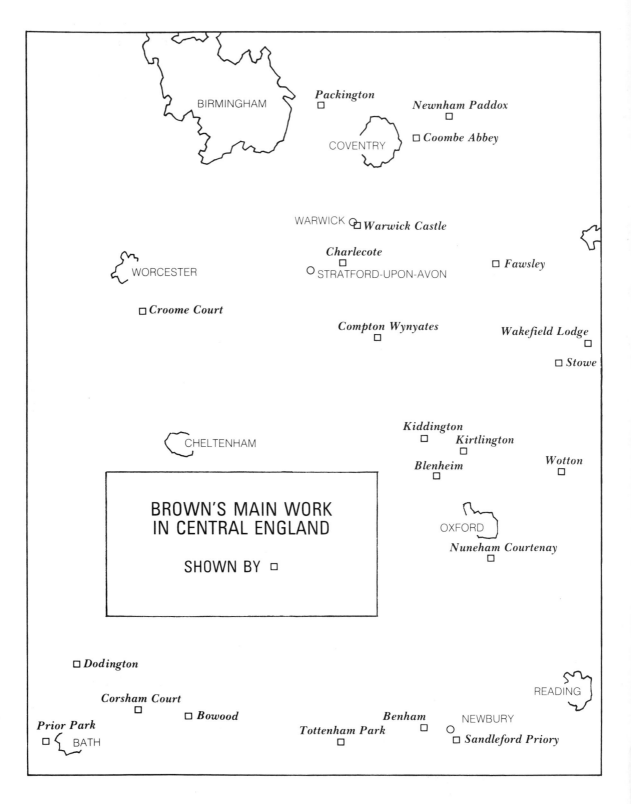

BROWN'S MAIN WORK
IN CENTRAL ENGLAND

SHOWN BY □

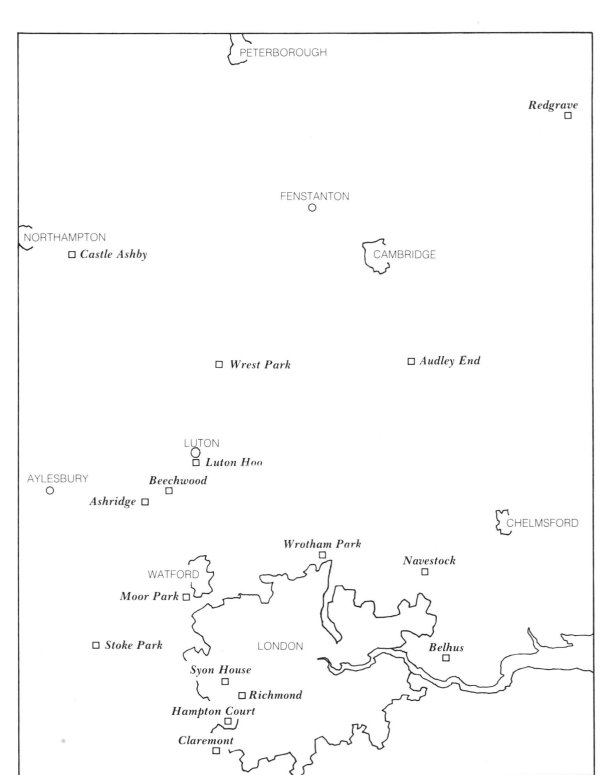

PETERBOROUGH

Redgrave □

FENSTANTON
○

NORTHAMPTON
□ *Castle Ashby*

CAMBRIDGE

□ *Wrest Park*

□ *Audley End*

LUTON
○
□ *Luton Hoo*

AYLESBURY
○

Beechwood
□

Ashridge □

CHELMSFORD

Wrotham Park
□

WATFORD

Navestock
□

Moor Park □

□ *Stoke Park*

LONDON

Belhus
□

Syon House
□

□ *Richmond*

Hampton Court
□

Claremont
□

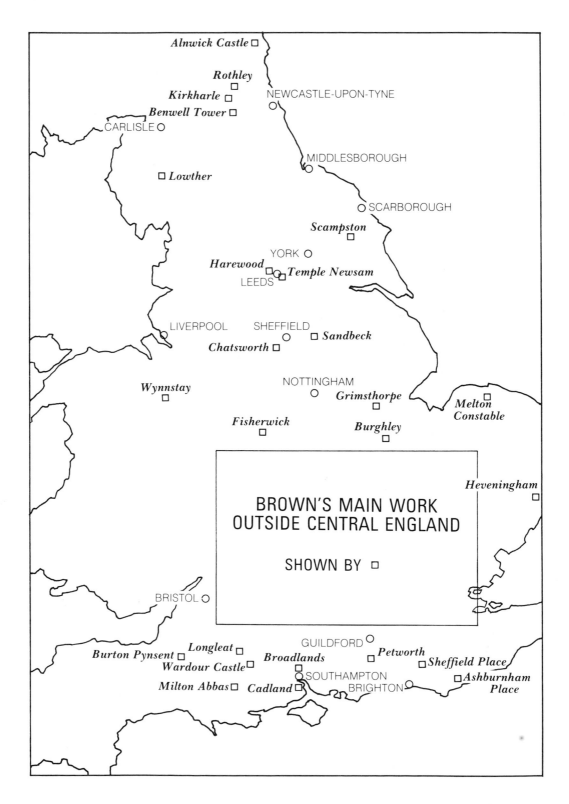

Alnwick Castle □

Rothley □

Kirkharle □   NEWCASTLE-UPON-TYNE

Benwell Tower □   □

CARLISLE ○

□ *Lowther*   MIDDLESBOROUGH ○

SCARBOROUGH ○

Scampston □

YORK ○

Harewood □ □ *Temple Newsam*
LEEDS

LIVERPOOL   SHEFFIELD ○
○   □ *Sandbeck*
           Chatsworth □

NOTTINGHAM
Wynnstay □   ○   *Grimsthorpe* □   *Melton Constable* □

Fisherwick □   *Burghley* □

Heveningham □

BROWN'S MAIN WORK
OUTSIDE CENTRAL ENGLAND

SHOWN BY □

BRISTOL ○

GUILDFORD ○
Longleat □   *Petworth* □
Burton Pynsent □   *Broadlands* □   *Sheffield Place* □
Wardour Castle □   SOUTHAMPTON ○   *Ashburnham Place* □
Milton Abbas □ *Cadland* □   BRIGHTON ○

Notes

BL = British Libarary, HMC = Historical Manuscripts Commission, PRO = Public Records Office, VCH = Victoria County History.

Chapter 1. Northumberland

1. Kirkharle Parish Baptismal Register, 1695-1751, Northumberland County Records Office, EP 127/1.
2. John Hodgson, *A History of Northumberland*, Part 2, I (1827), p. 243.
3. Kirkharle Parish Baptismal Register, as above.
4. John Hodgson, op. cit. p. 243.
5. *An Account of the Genealogy and other Memoirs Concerning the Family of Loraine*, printed John White, 1740, reprinted in *Reprints of Rare Tracts*, M.A. Richardson, 1849, biographical vol.II, pp. 18 and 19.
6. John Hodgson, op. cit. p. 243.
7. Sir Lambton Loraine, *Pedigree and Memoirs of the Family of Loraine*, 1902, p. 129.
8. Ibid., pp. 116 and 118.
9. Letter to the author.
10. John Hodgson, op. cit., pp. 249-50.
11. See Peter Willis, 'Capability Brown in Northumberland', *Journal of the Garden History Society*, 1981.
12. In the possession of John Anderson, to whom I am grateful for assistance.
13. John Hodgson, op. cit. pp. 249-50.
14. Peter Willis, op. cit.
15. John Wallis, *The Natural History and Antiquities of Northumberland*, 1769, II, p. 532.

Chapter 2. Stowe

1. I am indebted to Dr O.M. Brown for this information. He has pointed out that the second of these Smiths, the one Dorothy Stroud (in *Capability Brown*, 1950, revised editions 1957, 1975, 1984) identifies as Brown's probable contact in the south, could not have been Lady Loraine's ninety-year-old father, as she suggests, since his tombstone states

that when he died in 1742 he was fifty-two.
2. John Hodgson, op. cit., Part 2, I, p. 243.
3. J. Penn, *An Historical and Descriptive Account of Stoke Park*, 1813.
4. Ibid., p. 34.
5. Ibid., pp. 34-5.
6. William Mason, *Satirical Poems*, with notes by Horace Walpole.
7. G.B. Clarke, 'The History of Stowe, Part 14', *The Stoic*, December 1971, p. 17.
8. *Dictionary of National Biography*.
9. Information from the Stowe Collection at the Huntingdon Library, supplied by G.B. Clarke, who is presently revising his *History of Stowe*.
10. Horace Walpole, *History of the Modern Taste in Gardening*, 1780.
11. See G.B. Clarke, 'The History of Stowe, Part 8', *The Stoic*, Dec 1969. Levens Hall in Cumbria also claims to have the earliest English ha-ha. The first description of a simple ha-ha, consisting of a gap in a wall with a ditch, was published by Alexandre Le Blond in 1709.
12. Letter, Sir Thomas Robinson to Lord Carlisle, 23 December 1734, H.M.C., Carlisle MSS.
13. Jonathan Richardson, *Essays*, 1725.
14. *A Dialogue upon the Gardens of the Right Honourable the Lord Cobham at Stowe in Buckinghamshire*, 1848, printed J. and J. Rivington, pp. 28-9.
15. *The Tatler*, No. 123, 21 January 1710.
16. G.B. Clarke, 'The History of Stowe, Part 10', *The Stoic*, July 1970, p. 115.
17. *A Dialogue upon the Gardens...at Stowe*, op. cit., p. 21.
18. G.B. Clarke, op. cit., pp. 116-7.
19. Ibid., p. 120.
20. Thomas Whately, *Observations on Modern Gardening*, 1771, pp. 225-6. Whately's main interest was politics. He became a close friend of Cobham's nephew, George Grenville, the future Prime Minister, supplying him with an 'abundance of political gossip' (DNB).
21. Margaret Lady Verney, *Verney Letters of*

the Eighteenth Century, 1930, II, p. 129.

22. Four issues of November and December 1742, printed over the name of the new steward, L. Lloyd.

23. G.B. Clarke, 'The History of Stowe, part 14', op. cit., p. 20. I am grateful to Mr Clarke for this and many other suggestions in my treatment of Stowe.

24. The Stowe Collection at the Huntington Library.

25. Quoted by G.B. Clarke, 'The History of Stowe, Part 14', op. cit., p. 20.

26. Sir Henry Steuart, *The Planters' Guide*, 1827, 3rd edition, 1848, pp. 32-4.

27. Christopher Hussey, introduction to Dorothy Stroud, *Capability Brown*, 1984 edition, p. 30.

28. Found by David Easton.

29. J. Penn, op. cit., p. 35.

30. G.B. Clarke's estimate. See 'The History of Stowe, Part 14,' op. cit., p. 21.

Chapter 3. On Loan

1. Margaret Lady Verney, op. cit., II, p. 190.

2. Temple-Grenville Muniments at the Huntington Library. Richard Earl Temple's Personal Account, 1732-79, records small payments but they could have been tips for showing Grenville's guests round Stowe.

3. In the possession of the present Lady Denbigh, to whom I am grateful for assistance.

4. Historical Manuscripts Commission, Denbigh, Part 5. Letter from Cobham's sister, Hester Grenville, 15 Sept 1743.

5. Dorothy Stroud, op. cit., p. 54.

6. Margaret Lady Verney, op. cit., p. 235.

7. 'Building Book'.

8. *The Beautiful Lady Craven*, A.M. Broadley and Lewis Melville ed., 1826, I, pp. 34-5.

9. Joseph Cradock, *Literary and Miscellaneous Memoirs*, 1828, I, p. 157.

10. Ibid., IV, p. 187.

11. Ibid., IV, p. 187.

12. Horace Walpole, *Visits to Country Seats*, Walpole Society, XVI, p. 63.

13. George Gilbert Scott, *Personal and Professional Recollections*, 1879, p. 2.

14. *Stowe, A Guide to the Gardens*, 1974.

15. Lady Margaret Verney, op. cit., p. 200.

16. *Correspondence of Horace Walpole*, W.S. Lewis and Ralph S. Brown ed., 1941, IX, p. 121.

17. *Correspondence of Thomas Gray*, P. Toynbee and L. Whibley ed., 1935, I, p. 409.

18. 'Pakenham Correspondence' quoted in Dorothy Stroud, op. cit., pp. 62-3.

19. Letter dated 20 May 1766, Warwickshire County Records Office.

20. Warwickshire County Records Office.

21. *Correspondence of Horace Walpole*, ed. cit., XX, p. 302.

22. Ibid., XXIX, p. 303.

23. Ibid., XXIX, p. 260.

24. *An Eighteenth Century Correspondence*, Lilian Dickins and M. Stanton ed., 1910, p. 114.

25. Ibid., p. 162.

26. Ibid., quoted on p. 85.

27. William Dean, *Croome D'Abitot*, 1824, p. 38.

28. *An Eighteenth Century Correspondence*, op. cit., p. 214.

29. Dorothy Stroud, op. cit., p. 64, gives Sanderson Miller's diary as the source of this information, at present being edited by Anthony Wood.

30. *An Eighteenth Century Correspondence*, op. cit., p. 173.

31. Ibid., p. 184.

32. Property of the Trustees, Croome Settled Estates.

33. 'Pakenham Correspondence', quoted by Dorothy Stroud, op. cit., pp. 59-60.

34. Durham County Record Office, Strathmore Collection, D/St 347/37.

Chapter 4. His Own Man

1. Letter to Repton, 24 April 1792. Quoted, Humphry Repton, *Sketches and Hints on Landscape Gardening*, 1795, p. 14.

2. J. Townsend, *The Oxfordshire Dashwoods*, 1922, p. 24.

3. Ibid., p. 29.

4. Dashwood MSS (2), flyleaves for 1751 and 1752, and October 1752. See R.J. Robson, *The Oxfordshire Election of 1754*,

1949, p. 9.

5. J. Townsend, op. cit., p. 28.

6. This claim is also made for oaks planted near Cranbourne Lodge in Windsor Great Park in 1580.

7. V.C.H. for Oxfordshire, and unpublished notes by Christopher Buxton, the present owner.

8. Horace Walpole, *Memoirs of the Reign of George III*, 1894 edition, I, p. 215.

9. *Petworth House*, National Trust guide, 1984.

10. Petworth Archives.

11. By an unknown artist, in the Duke of Rutland's collection.

12, 13. Petworth Archives.

14. I am grateful to Geoffrey Binnie, M.A., F.I.C.E., F.R.S. for advice about earth dams and about Grundy's work, and to J.E. Taylor of Leconfield Estate Company for information about Petworth's dam.

15.-18. Petworth Archives.

19. 'Pakenham Correspondence', letter of 26 September 1753, quoted by Dorothy Stroud, op. cit., pp. 69-70.

20. Moor Park Handbook.

21. *Correspondence of Horace Walpole*, ed. cit., X, p. 285.

22. Dorothy Stroud, op. cit., p. 70.

23. 'Pakenham Correspondence', quoted by Dorothy Stroud, op. cit., p. 70.

24. *An Eighteenth-Century Correspondence*, op. cit., p. 226.

25. Ibid., p. 87.

26. Ibid., p. 111.

27. Ibid., p. 115.

28. Ibid., p. 366.

29. Ibid., p. 136.

30. Ibid., p. 226.

31. Ibid., p. 401.

32. Ibid., p. 416.

33. Dacre's account at Drummonds Bank.

34. VCH.

35. 'Pakenham Correspondence', quoted by Dorothy Stroud, op. cit., p. 74.

36. VCH.

37. *Harcourt Papers*, E.W. Harcourt ed., 1880-1905, VIII, p. 266.

38. Daniel Defoe, *Tour through England and Wales*, 1724-26, 1962 edition, II, p. 106.

39. *The Life of Robert Owen. Written by himself*, 1857-8.

40. *Correspondence of Horace Walpole*, ed. cit., IX, p. 184 and X, pp. 344-6.

41. *An Eighteenth-Century Correspondence*, op. cit., pp. 334-5.

42. Thomas Blore, *Guide to Burghley House*, 1815.

43. *Correspondence of Horace Walpole*, ed. cit., X, p. 344.

44. Burghley accounts.

45. *A History of Burghley House*, 1797, printed by J. and N. Eddowes, p. 189.

46. Ibid., p. 190.

47. 'Pakenham Correspondence', quoted by Dorothy Stroud, op. cit., p. 78.

48. Brown's account at Drummonds Bank.

49. Burghley accounts.

50. Ibid.

51. Ibid.

52. Eric Till, 'Capability Brown at Burghley', *Country Life*, 16 October, 1975. Dr Till attributes the staircase to Thomas Lumby after Adam. Dorothy Stroud claimed that it was Brown's. A further article, this one on the park and gardens at Burghley, is due to be published by Dr Till shortly, and I am grateful to him for letting me see this and for many suggestions in my account of Brown's work there.

53. *A History of Burghley House*, op. cit., p. 192.

54. There are four versions. The Burghley version is described in the 1815 guide as a copy.

55. Brown's account at Drummonds Bank.

Chapter 5. Fame

1. Percy FitzGerald, *The Life of David Garrick*, 1868, I, p. 396.

2. Alice Fairfax-Lucy, *Charlecote and the Lucys*, 1958, p. 204.

3. Warwickshire County Records Office.

4. Ibid.

5. Alice Fairfax-Lucy, op. cit., p. 225. The contract is lost but a later Lucy, Mary Elizabeth, quoted it in detail.

6. Ibid., p. 178.

7. Mrs Hayes' housebook, Warwickshire County Records Office.

8. Ibid.
9. Warwickshire County Records Office.
10. Alice Fairfax-Lucy, op. cit., p. 225.
11. Mrs Hayes' housebook.
12. Warwickshire County Records Office. Mr Langton's house was Newton Park in Somerset.
13. Warwickshire County Records Office.
14. Ibid.
15. At Longleat.
16. Daphne Bath, *Longleat*, 1949, p. 37.
17. R. Rigby to the Duke of Bedford, 3 February 1757.
18. Horace Walpole, *Memoirs of the Reign of George III*, ed. cit., II, pp. 126-7.
19. Ibid., III, p. 96.
20.-24. Longleat Archives.
25. Horace Walpole, *Visits to Country Seats*, ed. cit., XVI.
26. Essex County Records Office, Dacre Correspondence.
27. Cobham's personal account book, 21 March 1721.
28. Information supplied by G.B. Clarke. See chapter 2, note 9.
29. Horace Walpole, *Memoirs of the Reign of George III*, ed. cit., II, p. 115.
30. Ibid., I, p. 27.
31. Temple-Grenville Muniments, Huntington Library.
32. Ibid.
33. Thomas Whately, op. cit., pp. 84-7.
34. Dorothy Stroud, op. cit., p. 53, says sold to America in the 1930s, but Gordon Nares in 'Wotton House II', *Country Life*, July 8 1949, describes it as still at Wotton.
35. Dorothy Stroud, op. cit., p. 121.
36. *Correspondence of Horace Walpole*, ed. cit., XVI, p. 42.
37. VCH
38. Francis Epinasse, *Lancashire Worthies*, 1874, p. 269.
39. *Correspondence of Horace Walpole*, ed. cit., XXXV, p. 163.
40. See Francis Epinasse, op. cit., p. 271. The Earl of Chesterfield, in a letter to his son (1892 edition, IV, p. 326) implies that it was Elizabeth who broke off the engagement so that she could marry the Duke of Argyll.
41. VCH
42. Horace Walpole, *Visits to Country Seats*, ed. cit., XVI, p. 65.
43. Chatsworth account book, 1755-1765.
44. Oliver Gilbert, 'The Capability Brown Lawn and its management', *Landscape Design*, December 1983.
45. Dorothy Stroud, op. cit., introduction by Christopher Hussey, p. 35.
46. Dorothy Stroud, op. cit., pp. 88-9.
47. Corsham Archives at the Wiltshire County Records Office.
48. Ibid.
49. Ibid.
50. Alnwick, Ashridge, Aynho, Beechwood, Bowood, Burghley, Burton Constable, Charlecote, Chatsworth, Chillington, Cole Green, Corsham, Croome, Garrick's Villa, Harewood, Ingestre, Kirtlington, Longleat, Madingley, Moor Park, Newnham Paddox, Newton Park, Packington, Petworth, Ragley, Shortgrove, Spring Hill, Stoke House, Stowe, Syon House, Trentham, Wakefield, Warwick, Widdicombe, Wotton, Wrest. List compiled from Dorothy Stroud, op. cit.

Chapter 6. Royal Gardener

1. The Earl of Kerry, 'Bowood Park', *Wiltshire Archaeological and Natural History Magazine*, XLII, December 1924.
2. Brown's account book.
3. Quoted in *Lord Shelburne, the Bowood Circle and the American Revolution*, Oxford University Press, 1976, p. 4.
4. This and the following quotations from Lady Shelburne's diary in the Bowood Archives.
5. It hangs at Bowood.
6. Eton College Registers 1761-5.
7. Leeds Archives Department, Temple Newsam Archives, 25 November 1758.
8. 'Pakenham Correspondence', quoted by Dorothy Stroud, op. cit., p. 116.
9. Quoted Dorothy Stroud, op. cit., p. 117.
10. Leeds Archives Department, Temple Newsam Archives.
11. Ibid.

12. Audley End Handbook, 1984, p. 62.

13. Letter of 1 November 1765, at Essex County Records Office, D/DBy C/8/62.

14. Nikolaus Pevsner, *The Buildings of England: Essex*, 1965.

15. Schedule of work at the Essex County Records Office.

16. All the Griffin/Brown documents and correspondence quoted are at the Essex County Records Office, D/DBy A365.

17. Brown's account book.

18. Dorothy Stroud, op. cit., p. 113.

19. Horace Walpole, *Memoirs of the Reign of George III*, ed. cit., I, pp. 332-3.

20. *Correspondence of Horace Walpole*, ed. cit., XX, p. 341.

21. George Tate, *The History of the Borough, Castle and Barony of Alnwick*, 1866-9, I, p. 281.

22. A.M.W. Stirling, *Annals of a Yorkshire House*, I, p. 281.

23. George Tate, op. cit., I, p. 358.

24. Maiden Early, Copt Hall and Redgrave.

25. R. and J. Dodsley, *London and its Environs*, 1761, VI, pp. 11-13.

26. PRO works 6-8.

27. PRO works 6-13.

28. Brown's account book.

29. At Cambridge University Library.

30. PRO works 4-14 and 15, and 'Pakenham Correspondence', quoted by Dorothy Stroud, op. cit., p. 125.

31. *Annual Obituary*, III, p. 283.

32. E. Law, *History of Hampton Court Palace*, 1891, p. 297.

33. PRO works 4-15.

34. *Notes and Queries*, series 1, XII, p. 404.

35. E. Law, op. cit., p. 299.

36. PRO works 4-15 and works 1-4.

37. PRO works 1-4.

38. BL Additional MS 4113376.

39. The design for the Alhambra was probably by Johann Muntz. See John Harris, *Sir William Chambers*, 1970.

40. At Kew Library. Other versions at Windsor in the Royal Library and at PRO works 32-96.

41. PRO works 4-13.

42. Chatham MSS, PRO 30/8-24.

43. Milliken's letters, in the possession of a relative, quoted in Dorothy Stroud, op. cit., pp. 126-7.

Chapter 7. The Excellence of Blenheim

1. François de la Rochefoucauld, *Mélanges sur l'Angleterre*, 1784.

2. William Thackeray, *The Four Georges*, 1888.

3. The Earl of Cardigan, *The Wardens of Savernake Forest*, 1949, pp. 281-2.

4.-20. Savernake Archives, at the Wiltshire County Records Office, Ailesbury, 1300/1910 — 3266.

21. *Correspondence of Horace Walpole*, ed. cit., XII, p. 253.

22. Quoted by Hal Moggridge, 'Blenheim Park', *The Garden*, November 1983, p. 433.

23. *Correspondence of Horace Walpole*, ed. cit., XII, p. 253.

24. Sir James Prior, *Life of Edmond Malone*, 1860, pp. 406-7.

25. *Correspondence of Horace Walpole*, ed. cit., XXXII, p. 148.

26. Thomas Whately, op. cit., pp. 78 and 81.

27. BL, Add. MSS 5726. c.c. 72.

28. Hal Moggridge, to whom I am indebted for many suggestions in my description of Blenheim.

29. William Mavor, *A New Description of Blenheim*, 1789, pp. 99 and 3-4.

30. *Poetry and Prose of William Blake*, Geoffrey Keynes ed., 1927. Margin note to 'Reynold's Discourses', p. 981.

31. He was still Mr Lancelot Brown in March 1765. In May 1765, when a new page was begun for his account, he was Lancelot Brown Esq. An illegible margin note of 9 April seems to include the word Esq. I am grateful to Mr B. Cooper, and to Drummonds Bank for their assistance.

32. John Byng, *The Torrington Diaries*, C. Bruyn Andrews ed., 1934-8, I, p. 235.

Chapter 8. Lord of the Manor

1. Sir George Otto Trevelyan, 'Wallington I', *Country Life*, 22 June 1918.

2. John Hodgson, op. cit., part 2, I, pp.

249-50.

3. With the National Trust at Wallington.

4. John Hodgson, op. cit., part 2, I, pp. 249-50.

5. Rothley Castle by Daniel Garrett and Codger Fort by Thomas Wright.

6. Arthur Young, *A Six Months Tour through the North of England*, 1770, III, p. 94.

7. James Paine, *Plans, Elevations and Sections of Noblemen's and Gentlemen's Houses*, 1783, I, p. 14.

8. Mark Girouard, 'Sandbeck Park, Yorkshire', *Country Life*, 21 October 1965.

9. Brown's account book.

10. Letter to her aunt, quoted by Mark Girouard, op. cit.

11. *Correspondence of Horace Walpole*, ed. cit., I, p. 275.

12. Contract preserved at Sandbeck.

13. William Gilpin, *Observations Relating Chiefly to Picturesque Beauty*, 1776.

14. *Correspondence of Horace Walpole*, ed. cit., XXXVII, p. 438.

15. Ibid., XXI, p. 200.

16. Ibid., XIX, p. 419.

17. Ibid., XX, p. 345.

18. Ibid., IX, p. 153 and XXII, p. 311.

19. Ibid., XXV, p. 273.

20. MS letter, Hon Audrey Townshend to her father. Quoted ibid., XXXV, p. 246.

21. Both plans at East Sussex County Records Office, as are John Elphick's map of 1737 and J. Pennington's of 1797.

22. *Correspondence of Horace Walpole*, ed. cit., XXV, p. 414 and XXIX, p. 306.

23. Ibid., XXXIII, p. 184.

24. MS Journals, Coke, 10 June 1780. See *Correspondence of Horace Walpole*, ed. cit., XXXIII, pp. 184-5.

25. *Correspondence of Horace Walpole*, ed. cit., XXXIII, p. 175.

26. See Evelyn's *Diary*, 18 July 1687, which suggests that they were already being made.

27. *The Complete Letters of Lady Mary Wortley Montagu*, R. Halsband ed., 1965-67, III, p. 195.

28. Brown's account book.

29. Compton Family Archives at Castle Ashby, by permission of the Marquess of Northampton, 993.

30. Ibid., 1118.

31. Sixth Marquess of Northampton, *History of the Comptons of Compton Wynyates*, London, 1930, p. 197. The second comment is quoted from Nichols's *Literary Anecdotes of the Eighteenth Century*.

32. Compton Family Archives, 993.

33. Ibid. These figures are based on a graph prepared by Peter McKay from the monthly payrolls. I am grateful to Mr McKay for many other suggestions in my account of Castle Ashby.

34. Sixth Marquess of Northampton, op. cit., p. 197.

35. Compton Family Archives, 1118.

36. Ibid., letter dated 30 April, but year not given.

37. Ibid., 1118.

38. Ibid., 25 May 1767.

39. Ibid., 28 May 1767.

40. Ibid., 8 June 1767.

41. Ibid., 7 September 1767.

42. VCH.

43. Sixth Marquess of Northampton, op. cit., p. 211.

44. *Correspondence of Horace Walpole*, ed. cit., XXIII, p. 350.

45. Joseph Cradock, *Literary and Miscellaneous Memoirs*, 1828. Other information about Sandwich from same source, unless otherwise identified.

46. *Oxford English Dictionary*.

47. *Correspondence of Horace Walpole*, ed. cit., XXIII, p. 350.

48. Ibid., X, p. 153 and XXXVIII, p. 363.

49. Ibid., XXII, p. 312.

50. 'Pakenham Correspondence', quoted by Dorothy Stroud, op. cit., p. 170.

51. *Correspondence of Horace Walpole*, ed. cit., XXIX, p. 43.

52. *Town and Country Magazine*, 16 May 1773.

53. *The Beautiful Lady Craven*, op. cit., I, p. 32.

54. By Samuel Mathias, a Warwickshire surveyor.

55. 'Pakenham Correspondence', quoted

by Dorothy Stroud, op. cit., p. 177.
56. John Byng, *The Torrington Diaries*, ed. cit., II, p. 113.
57. Lincolnshire Archives Committee.

Chapter 9. Brown versus Chambers

1. At Blenheim, Chambers made the Bladon Bridge, the temples of Diana and Flora and the Bennini obelisk (John Harris, op. cit., p. 198).
2. Dorothy Stroud, *Henry Holland*, 1966, p. 22. Henry junior is not mentioned in the Holland building firm's records till 1767.
3. Quoted by Humphry Repton in *Observations on the Theory and Practice of Landscape Gardening*, 1803, pp. 168-9.
4. National Trust guide to Claremont, 1984, p. 23.
5. Humphry Repton, op. cit.
6. Accounts at the Soane Museum. Quoted by Phyllis M. Cooper in *The Story of Claremont*, 1983, p. 15.
7. T.B. Macaulay, *Essay on Clive*.
8. Francis Kilvert, *Kilvert's Diary*, William Plomer ed., 1938. Diary entry in 1871.
9. Claremont accounts.
10. Brown's account book, and Clive MSS, National Library of Wales.
11. 'Pakenham Correspondence', quoted Dorothy Stroud, *Capability Brown*, ed. cit., p. 168.
12. This was Chambers's second book on Chinese gardening. The first, *Of the Art of Laying Out Gardens Among the Chinese*, had been published in 1757.
13. William Chambers, *Dissertation on Oriental Gardening*, 1972 edition, John Harris ed., p. iii. First published in 1772.
14. *Correspondence of Horace Walpole*, ed. cit., IX, p. 121.
15. William Chambers, *Dissertation on Oriental Gardening*, ed. cit., p. 11.
16. Ibid., p. x.
17. Ibid., p. 14.
18. Ibid., pp. 36-8.
19. Ibid., pp. 35-6.
20. *Correspondence of Horace Walpole*, ed. cit., XXVIII, pp. 28-9. Chambers had been made a Knight of the Polar Star by the King of Sweden, then allowed by George III to assume his knighthood in England.
21. *Correspondence of Horace Walpole*, ed. cit., XXVIII, p. 34.
22. BL Add. MS 41 134, quoted by John Harris in *Sir William Chambers*, op. cit., p. 161.
23. Joseph Cradock, op. cit., IV, pp. 37-8.
24. *An Heroic Epistle to Sir William Chambers*, 1772, lines 55-62.
25. Ibid., lines 72-8.
26. Dorothy Stroud, *Capability Brown*, ed. cit., p. 160.
27. William Chambers, *Dissertation on Oriental Gardening*, 1773 edition, p. 157.
28. William Mason, *English Flower Garden*, Book 4, lines 178-82.
29. Horace Walpole, *Notes on Mason's Satires*, 1926 edition, p. 45.
30. Oliver Goldsmith, 'The Deserted Village'.
31. Horace Walpole, *Last Journals*. October 1773.
32. *Correspondence of Horace Walpole*, ed. cit., XXII, p. 498.
33. Brown's account book.
34. BL, Add. MS 41 136.
35. Ibid.
36. Ibid.
37. Arthur Oswald, 'Market Town into Model Village', *Country Life*, 29 September 1966.
38. *Diary and Letters of Madam d'Arblay*, Charlotte Frances Barrett ed., 1842-6, 1891 edition, III, p. 358.

Chapter 10. Brown for Pitt

1. Leeds Public Library Archives Dept., Harewood House Archives.
2. Brown's account book lists four plans, but it is not clear whether or not these were made at the time of his first visit.
3. Harewood House guide, 1983.
4.-7. Harewood House Archives.
8. Brown's account book.
9.-13. Harewood House Archives.
14. Brown's account book.
15. James Marshall and Marie Louise Osborn Collection, Yale University Library.

16. Wardour Archives, by permission of John Arundell.
17. Ibid. I am grateful to Fiona Cowell for her research on Richard Woods and for many suggestions in my account of Wardour.
18. Wardour Archives.
19. 'Pakenham Correspondence', quoted by Dorothy Stroud, *Capability Brown*, ed. cit., pp. 98-9.
20. Ibid., p. 99.
21. Wardour Archives.
22. Brown's account book and his account at Drummonds Bank.
23. *Notes of a Gardening Tour*, 1833.
24. Joseph Cradock, op. cit., II, p. 231.
25. John Nichols, *Literary Anecdotes of the Eighteenth Century*, 1812-15.
26. Philip Miller, *Gardener's Dictionary*, 1768.
27. Letter from Mainwaring to Brown, 21 August 1773, 'Pakenham Correspondence', quoted by Dorothy Stroud, *Capability Brown*, ed. cit., p. 172.
28. Letter from Brown to George Rice of Newton Castle, August 1775, Dyneover Castle Archives, quoted by Dorothy Stroud, *Capability Brown*, ed. cit., pp. 180-1.
29. Arthur Oswald, 'Scampston Hall, Yorkshire I', *Country Life*, 1 April 1954.
30. 'Pakenham Correspondence', 2 March 1773, quoted by Dorothy Stroud, *Capability Brown*, ed. cit., p. 174.
31. *Beauties of England and Wales*, Yorkshire Volume, 1812.
32. 'Pakenham Correspondence', quoted by Dorothy Stroud, *Capability Brown*, ed. cit., p. 173.
33. Records Office, Carlisle.
34. *Correspondence of Horace Walpole*, ed. cit., XXI, p. 527.
35. A.M.W. Stirling, op. cit., I, p. 285.
36. R.S. Ferguson, *The MPs of Cumberland and Westmorland*, 1871, p. 126.
37. A.M.W. Stirling, op. cit., p. 299.
38. De Quincey, *Collected Essays*, 1854, II, p. 254.
39. Alexander Carlyle, *Autobiography*, 1860, pp. 418-19.
40. A.M.W. Stirling, op. cit., p. 294.
41. Ibid., p. 318.
42. Ibid., p. 310.
43. Ibid., p. 312.
44. Ibid., p. 314.
45. 'Pakenham Correspondence', quoted by Dorothy Stroud, *Capability Brown*, ed. cit., p. 189.
46. Ibid.
47. *Harcourt Papers*, ed. cit.
48. All Brown-Pitt correspondence quoted from PRO, Chatham MSS 30/8-24, or from W.S. Taylor and J.H. Pringle, *Chatham Correspondence*, 1838-40, IV.

Chapter 11. Isis and Cam

1. *The Beautiful Lady Craven*, op. cit., II, p. 100.
2. 'Pakenham Correspondence', quoted by Dorothy Stroud, *Capability Brown*, ed. cit., p. 170.
3. Dorothy Stroud, *Henry Holland*, ed. cit., pp. 35-6.
4. East Sussex County Records Office, AMS 544/72.
5. *Dictionary of National Biography*.
6. Both at East Sussex County Records Office.
7. Mark Lower, *History of Sussex*, 1870.
8. *Correspondence of Horace Walpole*, ed. cit., XXIV, p. 328.
9. Ibid., XXXV, p. 460.
10. Mavis Batey, *Nuneham*, 1979, p. 6.
11. *Harcourt Papers*, ed. cit., III.
12. Letters Whitehead-Harcourt, July 1779.
13. Humphry Repton, op. cit., p. 219.
14. *Harcourt Papers*, ed. cit., VIII.
15. Mavis Batey, op. cit., p. 11.
16. Giles Worsley, 'Nuneham', *Country Life*, 10 January 1985.
17. *Diary and Letters of Madam d'Arblay*, ed. cit., II, pp. 126-35.
18. Correspondence of Horace Walpole, ed. cit., XXXIII, p. 417.
19. Ibid., XXIX, p. 88.
20. G. Dyer, *A History of the University and Colleges of Cambridge*, 1814, I, p. 234.
21. Ibid., I, p. 231.
22. Dorothy Stroud, *Capability Brown*, ed. cit., p. 182.
23. John Byng, *The Torrington Diaries*, ed.

cit., III, p. 176.

24. 'Northern Tour', Lord Verulam, Historical Manuscripts Commission.
25. *My Life and Times* by Nimrod (Apperley's pen-name).
26. Quotations from Wynn's and Chambre's letters, Wynn family papers, 122-5, at the National Library of Wales.
27. Brown's account book.
28. John Byng, *The Torrington Diaries*, ed. cit.
29. Ibid.
30. *Bye Gones*, (Bg) 1882, p. 133. The programme is quoted in full in 'An Architectural History of the Mansion of Wynnstay, Ruabon', *The Transactions of the Denbighshire Historical Society*, XXIX, 1980, by T.W. Pritchard, to whom I am grateful for assistance.

Chambre was finally dismissed for financial dishonesty, Wynn died five years later at the age of forty with debts of £160,000, the house was three times rebuilt, the last time after a great fire, and is now a school. Brown's dairy temple in the pleasure grounds survives (dilapidated) but the great Belan water is dry, its bed a birch thicket, the valley sides a jungle of young conifers.

Chapter 12. The Last Years

1. Hector Bolitho and Derek Peel, *The Drummonds of Charing Cross*, 1967, p. 70.
2. Peter Willis, 'Capability Brown's Account with Drummonds Bank, 1753-93', *Architectural History*, 1984.
3. John Ramsay of Ochtertyre, quoted by Bolitho and Peel, op. cit., p. 40.
4. Letter from Thomas Bradshaw, quoted by Bolitho and Peel, op. cit., p. 64.
5. Drummond Archives.
6. William Gilpin, *Remarks on Forest Scenery*, 1834 edition, II, pp. 217-18.
7. Drummond Archives.
8. *The Morning Chronicle and London Advertiser*, 12 July 1785.
9. The collection is called 'The Pakenham Correspondence' by Dorothy Stroud, who owns it.
10. 'Pakenham Correspondence', quoted Dorothy Stroud, *Capability Brown*, ed. cit., pp. 199-200.
11. *Correspondence of Horace Walpole*, ed. cit., XXXIII, p. 355.
12. Letter in the possession of the late Sir Eardley Holland, quoted Dorothy Stroud, *Capability Brown*, ed. cit., p. 196.
13. Mrs Montagu's letters quoted from Reginald Blunt, *Mrs Montagu, 'Queen of the Blues'*, 1925, pp. 109-23.
14. As note 12 above.
15. HMC, Bath, papers at Longleat.
16. PRO, PCC, Cornwallis, 108.
17. *Correspondence of Horace Walpole*, ed. cit., XXXIII, p. 285.
18. Ibid., XXIX, pp. 285-6.
19. Ibid., XXIX, p. 304.
20. Ibid., XXIX, p. 306.
21. Richard Payne Knight, *The Landscape*, 1794.
22. *Correspondence of Horace Walpole*, ed. cit., XXXIII, p. 366.
23. Quoted by Miles Hadfield, *Topiary and Ornamental Hedges*, 1971, p. 46.
24. 'Pakenham Correspondence', Dorothy Stroud, *Capability Brown*, ed. cit., p. 157.
25. *Letters of Hannah More*, Annette M.B. Meakin ed., 1911, p. 172.

Author's Acknowledgements

Among the many people who have helped me I would particularly like to thank John Anderson, John Arundell, Diana Baskerville-Glegg, Mavis Batey, the Revd J.D. Bickersteth, G.M. Binnie F.Eng., F.R.S., Judith Brent, Nancy Briggs, Dr O.F. Brown, Elaine Brunner, Christopher Buxton, the Earl of Cardigan, George Clarke, Fiona Cowell, Lady Denbigh, Pauline Dower, Mrs D.L. Maldwin Drummond, S.D.M. FitzGerald, Dr Susan Foister, Jane Fowles, Robin Gard, P.D. Grimes, Sheila Harvey, J.B. Henderson, Mrs James Legard, Alison McCann, Peter H. McKay, the Lord Maclean K.T., G.C.V.O., K.B.E., the Lord Methuen, Robin Moore, Hal Moggridge, G.R.A. Oliver, Brian Phillips, Canon T.W. Pritchard, Stuart Richmond-Wilson, Madge A. Robbins, the Baroness Robson, the Earl of Scarbrough, Dr Kenneth Saunders, the Earl of Shelburne, Colin Shrimpton, Dorothy Stroud, J.E. Taylor, Dr Eric Till, Peter Traskey, Stuart Wrathmell, the Revd J.K. Young.

Illustration Acknowledgements

The author and publishers would like to thank the museums, galleries, private collectors, photographers, photographic agencies and institutions who provided photographic material and kindly permitted its reproduction. Special thanks are due to Sir Geoffrey Agnew and Dr. Peter Willis.

Colour

The Trustees of the Croome Estate III; Property of Lord Forteviot on loan to Brooks's XVI (photography by Prudence Cummings Associates); Lord Harewood XXVII; Diana Saville XII, XIII. All other colour illustrations were commissioned from Timothy Beddow.

Black and white

Aerofilms Ltd. 45; Mr. John Anderson 4, 5 (photographs by John Young, Audio Visual Centre, University of Newcastle upon Tyne); Timothy Beddow, frontispiece, 2, 8, 10, 13, 14, 15, 16, 17, 18, 19, 20, 21, 22, 24, 26, 27, 28, 29, 30, 31, 34, 35, 39, 40, 41, 42, 46, 48, 49, 50, 51, 52, 54, 55, 56, 57, 59, 66, 68, 69, 70, 74, 75; Bodleian Library 11 (ref.28.552 Plate 3) and 44 (Gough Maps 26 fol.55B lower); Trustees of the British Museum 38; English Heritage 36; Property of Lord Forteviot on loan to Brooks's 73 (photograph by Prudence Cummings Associates); Lord Harewood 61, 62, 63; National Monuments Record 25, 32, 64, 65, 76; National Portrait Gallery 1, 7, 53, 58, 60, 67; The National Trust 47; Newcastle University Library 3; His Grace the Duke of Northumberland 37 (photograph by English Life Publications Ltd.); Oxfordshire County Libraries 71, 72; Diana Saville 33, 43; Sotheby's 77; Stowe School 9.

Index